Three-Minute Dramas for Worship

Karen Patitucci

Resource Publications, Inc. ● San Jose, CA

Editorial director: Kenneth Guentert
Production editor: Elizabeth J. Asborno
Art director: Ron Niewald

Library of Congress Cataloging in Publication Data

Patitucci, Karen.
    Three-minute dramas for worship / by Karen Patitucci.
        p.   cm.
    Includes indexes.
    ISBN 0-89390-143-1
    1. Christian drama. American.   I. Title.
PS3566.A776T48 1989
812'.54dc19   89-30342

5 4 3 2
93 92 91 90

With love and thanks to Stefan, Hannah, Marco, Thomas, and all the people of Hope for their support and encouragement.

Contents

The Hope Center Dream

The dream for Hope Center began in the mind of Jim Persson (currently director of Church Growth and Evangelism for the Evangelical Covenant Church of America). Jim reasoned that many people are not turned off by God as much as they are by the way He is presented.

Hope Center was designed to use the performing arts to communicate the truth. Contemporary music, drama, and multi-media are an integral part of all our Sunday celebrations.

A band with keyboards, bass, drums, and guitar plays the music at Hope Center. The music varies from traditional to rock with country and jazz in between. There are two songs that are thematic in each celebration; that is, they reiterate the morning theme. These songs are sung by three to six of the forty singers who are involved in the music ministry on a rotating basis.

The Sunday morning dramas also express the morning theme. Bringing biblical truth to life in the sketches is an entertaining way to communicate the focus of the celebration. Through the drama, people are given mental pictures of the truths they have heard. These pictures remain with them long after they've forgotten the details of what was said.

Multi-media is another way of creating drama in our celebrations. Hearing a song about hungry people may or may not be impressive. Hearing a song and simultaneously seeing pictures of hungry people will definitely solicit response.

For the past ten years, Hope Center has been using the performing arts to reach our community with the truth. Because good communication occurs through repetition, we have found the thematic music, drama, and multi-media an asset to the communication of gospel truths.

1
White Flag

Topic:
Anger

Theme:
It is not enough to read the Bible. We must learn to apply it in everyday situations.

Scripture:
Ephesians 4:26,27

Characters:
Wife
Hubby

Props:
dishtowel
a few dishes

Hubby and Wife are washing dishes.

WIFE: I'm going to bed.

HUBBY: You can't.

WIFE: Yes, I can, and I am.

HUBBY: Don't you remember what we read in our devotions this morning?

WIFE: *(She remembers but won't admit it.)* No! And I am not going to remember, either.

HUBBY: We read Ephesians 4. We decided we'd try to be more honest with one another and that we'd *never* go to bed angry.

WIFE: *(Determined not to remember)* I do not remember that.

HUBBY: We decided to memorize Ephesians 4:26. "Be angry, but do not sin. Do not let the sun go down on your anger." We felt that it would be good for our relationship.

WIFE: Yes, but we decided all that before we had this fight.

HUBBY: Well, if *you'd* just apologize everything would be fine.

WIFE: *(Very upset)* Me! It wasn't my fault! It's your fault. You're the one who started it.

HUBBY: I know, I know. *(Putting his hands up in the air)* I give up! I was just kidding. It's all my fault. I'm sorry.

WIFE: You're just saying that. You don't really mean it. You just want the fight to be over.

HUBBY: No. I really am sorry. It was just a little mistake.

WIFE: Little mistake?

HUBBY: I meant big, big mistake, a very big mistake.

WIFE: You don't sound very sincere.

HUBBY: I am, really. *(Ties dishtowel on to a utensil.)* It was my fault.

WIFE: What are you doing?

HUBBY: I'm making a white flag. I'm surrendering. This is my flag of truce. A graphic representation of our commitment to peace.

WIFE: You're crazy.

HUBBY: But I love you.

WIFE: I know.

HUBBY: Do you forgive me?

WIFE: Yeah. You know, maybe we should keep this flag in the kitchen. It'll probably come in handy.

HUBBY: You don't think we'd actually ever fight again?

WIFE: No, but just in case...

LIGHTS

2
Temperament Transformation

Topic:
Anger

Theme:
Everyone gets angry and most everyone has trouble dealing in a godly way with their anger. However, God wants to help people deal correctly with anger if they are willing to recognize and admit their problem.

Scripture:
Psalm 4:4,5
Matthew 5:22,24
Ephesians 4:26,27

Characters:
Man (an average male chauvinist)
Tina (enthusiastic but confrontative)
Terry (enthusiastic but confrontative)

The Temperament Transformation Center. Man enters slowly.

TINA: *(Cheerfully)* Can I help you?

MAN: *(Nervously)* Well, actually, I don't really want to be here. *(Awkward pause; Tina looks perplexed.)* My wife made me come. She thinks I need a temperament transformation.

TERRY: *(Bursting in, very bubbly, extroverted)* Did I hear that someone needs a temperament transformation? How wonderful! *(Shaking man's hand)* You've come to the right place, the Temperament Transformation Center. I'm Terry Tame and this is Tina, a Temperament Transformer Trainee. Now, what do you seem to be having trouble with? Depression? Anxiety? Hatred? Impulsiveness? *(Man shakes his head "no" each time.)*

TINA: His wife sent him.

TERRY: Then *you* must be having trouble with anger.

MAN: *(Defensively)* I don't have trouble with anger. My wife does.

TERRY: I see. Your name?

MAN: Robert Rageford.

TERRY: Sit right down, Mr. Rageford, and I'll get your file. *(Terry exits momentarily.)*

MAN: My file?

TINA: Well, you see we've been expecting you. In fact, during the last week, we've been filming you in order to pinpoint what types of anger you have.

TERRY: *(Re-entering)* And looking at this report, it appears you exhibit all five kinds of anger. We'll show you what we mean. *(Man sits.)* Last Saturday you were putting up shelves in the garage when you hit your thumb rather than the nail with the hammer. *(Man gets up, begins to hammer, pretends to hit his thumb.)*

MAN: *(Gets up, begins to hammer, hits his thumb. Yelling)* Ow, darn it all...*(Mumbles.)* RATS! *(Throws hammer.)*

TINA: You see, a perfect example of Anger Type One, instantaneous anger.

MAN: Well, it did hurt and I was mad.

TERRY: *(Patronizing)* We understand. Then on Sunday your wife took the kids to Marine World and you didn't want to go.

MAN: So?

TINA: Remember what happened when you went to the refrigerator?

(Man acts this out.)

MAN: There is nothing to eat in here. How could she leave me alone with no food, no sandwiches, nothing. I'll probably starve and she doesn't even care. She cares about the kids more than she does me. Boy, am I going to let her have it when she gets home.

TINA: A classic example of Anger Type Two. It occurs when we're feeling neglected, as you did.

MAN: You know, this whole thing makes me pretty mad.

What gives you the right to film me without my knowledge. *(Standing.)* You've violated my right to privacy. I could sue you for this. In fact, I think I will.

TERRY: Sit down, Mr. Rageford. You're exhibiting signs of our third type of anger, which is anger resulting from a violation of personal rights.

TINA: I guess we can skip the part where he gets angry at his son for using the last of the hairspray, and where he starts yelling at his wife for not putting the cap back on the toothpaste, and where he kicks the dog for going to the bathroom on the morning newspaper.

MAN: You've got all that on film?

TERRY: Yes, we do. The fourth type of anger is the kind you have when you fight with your wife. Remember Sunday afternoon?

MAN: Look, I'm not interested in seeing a film clip of me and my wife arguing. I know we fight; I get angry, big deal. I admit it.

TERRY: Good.

MAN: *(Defensively)* And now you're going to tell me I'm not a good husband because I throw things when we fight; well, at least I don't throw things at her. And just because I don't fight fair, that doesn't mean I'm not a good husband. You can't blame a guy for wanting to win, can you? Maybe I do some things wrong, but nobody's perfect.

TERRY: That makes you angry, doesn't it?

MAN: Yeah.

TERRY: That shows you've got our final kind of anger, performance anger. That means you get angry when you're not performing the way *you* think you should. You need a complete temperament transformation.

MAN: Wait a minute, are you telling me it's wrong to get angry?

TERRY: No, the feelings are okay. But sometimes the way you deal with the feelings is wrong.

MAN: Can you help me deal better with the feelings?

TINA: Sure. We've helped thousands of others.

TERRY: There are five steps you need to know in order to deal with your feelings.

1. Recognize and admit you are angry.
2. Respond to your feelings; don't give in to emotional reflex.
3. Ask God to help you deal responsibly with your anger.
4. Deal responsibly with it.
5. Practice this approach.

Now, let's get started.

LIGHTS

3
Backing It Up

Topic:
Apologetics

Theme:
How do we know the Bible is a reliable book? There is an enormous amount of historical evidence to confirm its reliability.

Scripture:
2 Timothy 3:16
2 Peter 1:20,21
Psalms 12:6,7

Characters:
Skeptic
Believer
Records
Resume
Recommendations

Props:
a large, cardboard Bible

Believer is reading Bible when Skeptic enters. The Bible is large (human size), so Records, Resume, and Recommendations will initially be hidden by it.

SKEPTIC: Are you reading your Bible *again?*

BELIEVER: I'm not *just* reading; I'm studying.

SKEPTIC: Why would anyone want to study a big, long, boring, fairy tale like the Bible?

BELIEVER: It's not boring, and it's not the fairy tale you seem to think it is.

SKEPTIC: You don't really believe that stuff, do you?

BELIEVER: It's the truth and if you were as intellectual as you claim to be, you'd read it before passing judgment. After all, this book has drawn more attention than any other. Don't you wonder why?

SKEPTIC: It's just a fairy tale.

BELIEVER: For your information, the Bible is a historical document.

SKEPTIC: *(Thinking Believer is kidding him)* Give me a break.

BELIEVER: It's the truth. Look behind the Bible and you'll find the three Rs of education backing it up.

SKEPTIC: *(Looks at Believer; looks at Bible.)* You don't really expect me to believe there's anything backing this up, do you? *(Looks behind Bible)* Hey, who are you?

RECORDS: We're the three Rs that back up the Bible.

SKEPTIC: Reading, writing, and 'rithmetic?

BELIEVER: *(Introducing characters)* This is Records, Resume, and Recommendation.

SKEPTIC: This is weird.

RECORDS: There is an enormous amount of bibliographical evidence to support that the Bible is an accurate, historical document.

SKEPTIC: How do I know you're telling the truth?

RECORDS: Well, if you're the intelligent person you claim to be, you'll check the records.

RESUME: Did you know that the Bible's resume includes that it was written by over forty different men from many different vocations, many who were eye witnesses to what they wrote about, *and* that there is one central theme throughout—God reaching man.

SKEPTIC: I didn't know there was any theme.

RESUME: And the men who wrote it were willing to die for what they believed.

SKEPTIC: I never really thought about that.

RECOMMENDATIONS: And don't forget that many people who set out to disprove the Bible became believers in the process.

BELIEVER: People have even tried to ban and destroy it.

RECOMMENDATIONS: But no one has, or will succeed. They've died, but God's Book continues to live.

SKEPTIC: I had no idea that all this was behind the Bible. But being the intelligent person that I am, I think I'll have a look inside. *(Goes behind book.)*

LIGHTS

4
I Can't Figure It Out

Topic:
Attitude

Theme:
God calls his people not only to do the right things, but to do them for the right reasons.

Scripture:
Galatians 6:7-10

Characters:
Jami
Laurie

Props:
a long list

Two friends are having coffee.

JAMI: I've been checking my attitude and it seems like everything should be great, but it's not.

LAURIE: What's wrong?

JAMI: Everything. I mean you'd think my husband and I would be getting along great, but we're fighting like crazy. It doesn't make sense because I'm a *very* forgiving person. I've forgiven Ken for everything he's ever done wrong. I forgave him for forgetting our anniversary; for washing my cashmere sweater in hot water; for calling my mother an old bat; for coming home late without calling; and even for taking money out of the automatic teller without telling me, which really made the checking account a ruin; not to mention *(pulls long list out of her pocket)* all these other things.

LAURIE: You've got quite a list.

JAMI: Well, my memory is not too good and I don't want to forget anything. So you can see I really am a forgiving person, and I'm a serving person too. Just last Saturday I watched Suzy's three *brats* for her even though I had better things to do; and I waste one Sunday a month visiting people I don't even know in a convalescent hospital; and I made dinner for the Carlsons when they brought their baby home from the hospital, and that was a lot of work, not to mention expense. And then I—

LAURIE: *(Interrupting)* Wait. I think I know what your problem is.

JAMI: What?

LAURIE: First of all, when you forgive somebody you're supposed to forget; otherwise it's not really forgiving. You've got a running list of everything your husband's ever done wrong. That shows you haven't really forgiven him. And, yes, you do help people, but you act like you're doing them this *big* favor. You aren't helping people because you want to, but because you think you should.

JAMI: But if I'm doing the right things, my attitude should be right.

LAURIE: No, you've got to have the right reasons for doing the right things to have the right attitude.

JAMI: Are you saying I've got to sow a right attitude to reap one, and I'll only do that if I start doing things for the right reasons?

LAURIE: Right.

JAMI: I suppose I could start by throwing away this list.

LAURIE: That would be an excellent start.

LIGHTS

5
Special Delivery

Topic:
Beatitudes: Pure In Heart

Theme:
The only way to see God and understand Him is to be pure in heart, to follow the instructions for life Jesus gave us, in particular, the beatitudes. Too often our own ideas keep us from seeing Him.

Scripture:
Matthew 5:8

Characters:
Hubby (Mr. Maguillicuddy)
Wife (Mrs. Maguillicuddy)
Messenger

Props:
package
three cardboard keys
clipboard
paper with instructions on it

In the Maguillicuddy's living room.

HUBBY: *(As if watching football game on TV)* Go, go! Touchdown! All right!

MESSENGER: *(Knocks on door; Hubby opens it.)* I have a special delivery package for Mrs. Maguillicuddy.

HUBBY: Where do I sign?

MESSENGER: *You* don't. I am only allowed to release this package to the addressee.

HUBBY: Who's it from?

MESSENGER: The O.H.A.

HUBBY: What's that?

MESSENGER: The Office of Heavenly Affairs.

HUBBY: *(Yelling)* Honey, there's a package here from the Office of Heavenly Affairs.

WIFE: *(Very excited)* It's here. That's great. *(Entering)* Where do I sign?

MESSENGER: Number 26.

WIFE: Right. Thank you. Honey would you tip him? *(Walks away from messenger; shakes package.)* Wait until you see what's in here. I am so excited.

HUBBY: What did you order from the Office of Heavenly Affairs?

WIFE: It's incredible. *(Opening package)* It's God.

HUBBY: God? In a box?

WIFE: All we have to do is find the right key and then we'll see God. I know I've got the key here somewhere. You know, you should probably call the *Enquirer* and have them send a photographer. This is front-page material.

HUBBY: *(Thinking this must be a joke)* You're kidding me. You don't really believe you'll see God in that box.

WIFE: I'm not kidding. You don't think I've been involved in all those different ministries for the last five years for nothing, do you? Look here's the financial key. This should open the box. We've been tithing 17 per cent for two years now. That should definitely open the box.

HUBBY: *(A little irritated)* 17 per cent? You *are* kidding me, aren't you?

WIFE: *(Preoccupied with opening the box)* No. I'm not. What is wrong with this key? It's not working. 17 per cent and it's not working. I'll have to try another one. Don't worry. I'll use my attendance key. I haven't missed a service in five years, and I only missed Bible study once. That should open up this box.

HUBBY: I can't believe you've been tithing 17 per cent for two years and haven't told me.

WIFE: This key isn't working either.

HUBBY: 17 per cent? 17 per cent? That's ridiculous. Why on earth...?

WIFE: Honey, that really isn't important right now. What

is important is how we're going to get this open. We'll talk about the 17 per cent later. Now, will you help me?

HUBBY: Did you consider reading the directions? *(He picks up the directions and begins to read them.)*

WIFE: *(Looks at him blankly.)* I've got one more key— my good deeds, walking elderly people across the streets, buying girl scout cookies, working to save the whales, hummingbirds, and pink-antennae butterflies. *(Tries key.)* It doesn't fit. *(Disillusioned)* I can't believe it. I've worked so hard.

HUBBY: Do you want to know what the directions say?

WIFE: OK, what do they say?

HUBBY: Only the pure in heart will see God.

WIFE: The *pure* in heart?

HUBBY: That's right.

WIFE: *(Sighs, resigned)* Better wait on calling the *Enquirer.* I don't think I'm going to be able to get this box open today.

HUBBY: Right.

LIGHTS

6
The Light of the Book

Topic:
Bible

Theme:
The Bible is relevant to us today. It can show us reality, provide us with direction, and give us the power to follow that direction.

Scripture:
2 Peter 1:19-21
Psalms 119:105
Romans 1:16,17
Matthew 4:4

Characters:
Non-believer (female)
Believer (B)

Props:
two Bibles

Believer and Non-Believer are debating the relevance of the Bible.

NON-BELIEVER You don't really believe all that nonsense about the Bible, do you?

BELIEVER: Yes, I do.

NON-BELIEVER But it's just a book full of contradictions, erroneous information, and fairy tales.

BELIEVER: Weren't you listening to the message this morning? It's not just a book. It's sixty-six books, and it's not full of contradictions or erroneous information. In fact, it's provided information to scientists and histori—

NON-BELIEVER I know; I know. But let's face it. When it gets down to living in this modern world, it's got nothing relevant to say.

BELIEVER: Are you kidding? It's got everything relevant to say. It's the only Book that helps me see things as they really are.

NON-BELIEVER Are you crazy? If you take the Bible seriously, you'll be financially ruined. You can't lie, or cheat, or even mislead people. You might even tithe. Ten per cent may not be much now, but when I make my first million, there's no way I'm giving up $100,000.

BELIEVER: So you're going to let money guide your life?

NON-BELIEVER Money and a *perfect* husband. That's all I need. Then I'll be the *perfect* wife, we'll have *perfect* children and live the *perfect* life happily ever after.

BELIEVER: Not without the Bible.

NON-BELIEVER Oh, I'm going to use the Bible. After all, it's got all the criteria for a perfect husband. 1 Corinthians 13, Ephesians 5, 1 Peter 3...

BELIEVER: But you're only using a part of the instructions. Your "perfect" plan isn't going to hold together without all of them.

NON-BELIEVER Of course it will.

BELIEVER: *(Shaking head)* If you change your mind, don't forget to look in here. *(Exits with Bible open in hands, then closes it right before getting off stage. When Bible closes, the lights go out.)*

NON-BELIEVER I won't need it. Hey, what'd you do that for? Turn the lights back on. That's not funny. How can I do anything if it's dark? I'll be stumbling around like crazy! I tell you what, I'll give you $50 to turn on the lights. OK, $100. Please, I hate being in the dark. Maybe if I can just find that book. *(Stumbles a bit; finds the Book; opens it. Lights go on. Non- believer looks amazed; closes Book. Lights go off. Non-believer opens the Book; lights go on.)* Maybe there is something to this after all.

LIGHTS

7
Heavenly Stock Exchange

Topic:
Bible

Theme:
In order to gain the full benefit of God's Word, one must not only read it or listen to others talk about it, but also must study it. An investment of time and money is required.

Scripture:
2 Timothy 2:15
2 Timothy 3:16,17
Hebrews 4:12

Characters:
Stockbroker
Client

A brokerage office

CLIENT: You're my broker. You should be able to tell me what's going on with my investment.

STOCKBROKER: I can. And I want you to know that you are not alone in your concern.

CLIENT: I don't care whether I'm alone or not. I want to know if the bottom's dropped out.

STOCKBROKER: No, it hasn't. There's no need for you to panic. You are realizing your lack of dividends because of your limited investment. If you remember, I told you your portfolio needed to be diversified.

CLIENT: But I made a commitment to Christ, I try to get to church every week, I have a Bible, and occasionally I read it. You told me I'd have a secure investment.

STOCKBROKER: Your investment *is* secure. But you're not investing enough to get the spiritual dividends you really want.

CLIENT: I don't have anything more I want to invest.

STOCKBROKER: Then you won't get the dividends, the abundant life, the joy, the peace, the power—

CLIENT: OK, OK, OK. What would I need to invest?

STOCKBROKER: A little money and a lot of time.

CLIENT: But I'm busy.

STOCKBROKER: Then settle for the security and forget the benefits.

CLIENT: But I don't want just the security. What do I need to do to get the benefits?

STOCKBROKER: Study the Bible.

CLIENT: But I don't understand it. That's the minister's job. That's why I go to church.

STOCKBROKER: But you need to read it for yourself.

CLIENT: But I can't understand it.

STOCKBROKER: You haven't even tried. You need to get yourself a concordance, a bible dictionary, and a commentary. Then you need to sit down and study.

CLIENT: Study? But I haven't studied since college, and even then I didn't really study.

STOCKBROKER: If you want the benefits, you've got to make the investment.

CLIENT: It sounds so risky.

STOCKBROKER: It's the safest investment you can make. It's totally insured by the Holy Spirit.

CLIENT: *(A little hesitant)* OK. I'll make the investment.

STOCKBROKER: It looks like the spiritual indicator is rising.

CLIENT: I hope so.

LIGHTS

8
The Lawyer's Future

Topic:
Biblical Prophecy

Theme:
Biblical prophecy is one way God reveals Himself to man. It is a proclamation of truth that helps man see God. There is no way of denying it.

Scripture:
Luke 24:44

Characters:
Lawyer (egotistical, self-centered, arrogant; female)
First Assistant
Second Assistant

A lawyer's office

LAWYER: *(Proudly)* I have finally secured my future. My plans to discredit the Bible because of its false prophecies will get me success, new clients, perhaps even a political nomination. There will be reporters and photographers. I'll be a heroine—if only my two assistants come up with the necessary documentation I need to support my theories.

(On the opposite side of the stage are the assistants. They begin talking as the lawyer stops.)

FIRST ASSISTANT: What are we going to tell her?

SECOND ASSISTANT: The truth.

FIRST ASSISTANT: She's not going to like it.

SECOND ASSISTANT: What choice do we have? If we don't tell her now, she'll end up making a fool of herself in court and then we'll really be in trouble.

FIRST ASSISTANT: I suppose you're right, but she's going to be pretty upset with us.

SECOND ASSISTANT: What else is new?

FIRST ASSISTANT: Ready to face her?

SECOND ASSISTANT: As ready as I'll ever be.

(They walk over to the lawyer's office and knock.)

LAWYER: Come in. I was hoping it was you two. I certainly hope you have the information I need.

FIRST ASSISTANT: Well, actually, not exactly.

SECOND ASSISTANT: You see, the facts were not exactly the way you thought they'd be.

LAWYER: What *exactly* do you mean?

FIRST ASSISTANT: You know your first theory: that the entire Bible was written after Jesus' death?

LAWYER: Right. And the people who wrote the Bible made up the prophecies to support Jesus' claims.

SECOND ASSISTANT: That wasn't exactly possible.

LAWYER: What do you mean, wasn't *exactly* possible?

FIRST ASSISTANT: Well, historians have a copy of the Old Testament dated 250 B.C.

SECOND ASSISTANT: Which leaves a 250-year gap between the last prophecy and Jesus' birth.

LAWYER: *(Thinks a moment; paces a little.)* What about my second theory that Jesus purposely fulfilled the prophecies?

SECOND ASSISTANT: That couldn't *exactly* have happened either.

LAWYER: Why *exactly* couldn't it?

FIRST ASSISTANT: Some of the prophecies were out of Jesus' control, like the fact that he was born of a virgin.

SECOND ASSISTANT: Or that he would be born in Bethlehem.

LAWYER: *(She is obviously upset but tries to remain hopeful.)* I see your point. But what about my third theory that the fulfillment of the prophecies was just a series of coincidences?

FIRST ASSISTANT: Well, as you know, there are sixty major prophecies about the Messiah.

SECOND ASSISTANT: The odds that just eight of those coming true are, well, astronomical.

LAWYER: What *exactly* do you mean, "astronomical"?

FIRST ASSISTANT: You know the state of Texas?

LAWYER: Yes.

FIRST ASSISTANT: If you filled it two feet deep with silver dollars and marked one silver dollar with an X and then blindfolded somebody and asked them to pick up a silver dollar, the odds that he would pick up the marked silver dollar on the first try are the odds that eight of the prophecies were filled by coincidence.

LAWYER: I guess I had better rethink my future success. *(Getting an idea)* You know, I wonder if the Bible has anything to say about my future. That'll be your next project. Check out what the Bible says about my life. *(As assistants are exiting)* Never mind, you might get it wrong. I'll do it myself.

LIGHTS

9
Being Somebody

Topic:
Christmas

Theme:
The chaos of the holidays can crush the real spirit of Christmas. Caught up in the parties, programs, and shopping, we may begin to feel like nobodies. We need each other to reflect the joy that comes from remembering God's gift to us. Then we can realize we *are* somebodies.

Scripture:
John 3:16,17
Psalms 139:14-16
Ephesians 2:8-10

Characters:
Sales Clerk (female)
First Customer (crabby and irrational)
Second Customer (irritable and hard-headed)
Third Customer (friendly)

Sales Clerk is sincerely trying to maintain the spirit of Christmas, but is having a hard day. First and Second Customer are irrationally upset and irritable.

FIRST CUSTOMER: Do you work here?

SALES CLERK: Yes. May I help y—

FIRST CUSTOMER: It's about time I found someone who works here. You'd think with the prices you charge I'd be able to get a little help. I've wasted twenty minutes looking for a salesperson.

SALES CLERK: What can I help you with?

FIRST CUSTOMER: I need three Cabbage Patch dolls.

SALES CLERK: I'm sorry, but we've been out of those since Halloween.

FIRST CUSTOMER: *(Outraged)* How can you be out of them? You were out of them last year! I've got three daughters at home and they're expecting a Cabbage Patch doll. What am I going to tell them? And look here, I've already picked out a wardrobe of clothes for the dolls. You shouldn't be selling the clothes if you don't have the dolls to put them in. I'm going to talk to the manager about this.

SALES CLERK: *(Shrugs, not sarcastic, just disheartened))* Another happy shopper.

(Second Customer approaches sales clerk abruptly.)

SECOND CUSTOMER: I was charging some toys and apparently there is something the matter with my credit here. That clerk over there told me I had to go to the credit department. I won't go. I've shopped at this store for seven years and have never once been asked to go the credit department. It's humiliating. Why, she embarrassed me in front of several customers. Don't they teach clerks manners anymore? Anyway, I'm not going up there. I want you to call them and straighten this whole thing out over the telephone.

SALES CLERK: I don't think it will do any good, but I'll try. *(Picks up phone)* Hello, this is Cathy in the toy department, and Mr....Mr....*(Second Customer hands her his card)*...Mr. Grinch is here—

SECOND CUSTOMER: That's Grunch, not Grinch.

SALES CLERK: I'm sorry. Mr. Grunch is here and apparently we've made some sort of mistake with his card and he wants me to straighten—

SECOND CUSTOMER: *(Interrupting)* What exactly is the problem?

SALES CLERK: Uh-huh. I see. OK.

SECOND CUSTOMER: *(Grabs phone)* Listen, you either approve this purchase now, or forget me as a customer forever. Fine! Good-bye! *(Hangs up the phone; exits.)*

SALES CLERK: *(Looking heavenward)* I'm finding it a little difficult to maintain the true spirit of Christmas here.

THIRD CUSTOMER: *(Timidly to sales clerk)* Could you help me?

SALES CLERK: *(Happy to have a pleasant customer)* Sure. What can I do for you?

THIRD CUSTOMER: I'm looking for the boy's department. Now, I know this is the toy department but every person I've asked sends me here. I don't think they're listening. I've asked three salespeople and two customers. They're all so busy. Frankly, you're the first person today I've even seen smile. I was beginning to think people don't do that anymore. It's pretty difficult to maintain the Christmas spirit around here. I've only been here an hour and I already feel like a goldfish in a bowl of piranha. Everybody grabbing and pushing and shoving and complaining. It's enough to make anybody feel like a nobody.

SALES CLERK: I know exactly what you mean. I was beginning to feel like a nobody myself, that is until you came along. I try to remember the real spirit of Christmas. But it *can* be difficult in all this chaos.

THIRD CUSTOMER: Maybe that's why other people forget what this season is all about.

SALES CLERK: What do you mean?

THIRD CUSTOMER: Maybe they feel like a nobody, too. Maybe they forget that Jesus is God's gift to each of them.

SALES CLERK: Maybe we're supposed to be reminders that knowing God and realizing his gift makes a person somebody.

THIRD CUSTOMER: I think so. Now can you tell me how to get to the boy's department?

SALES CLERK: Of course.

LIGHTS

10
Equally Overboard

Topic:
Christmas

Theme:
Christians and non-Christians can be equally caught up in the busy-ness of Christmas. We must be careful that activities are not more important than the event itself.

Scripture:
John 1

Characters:
Mom
Child (Jenny)
Marge

A phone call between two friends

MOM: *(To Child, very irritated)* I'm on the phone. Go pick out a storybook and I'll read it to you as soon as I'm off the phone.

CHILD: But mom!

MOM: Go! Anyway, Marge, I've just been going absolutely crazy trying to make this Christmas the most memorable for my kids.

MARGE: Me too! I've been shopping until dropping. There are so many new toys out and I've been going to all the stores to make sure I get them. And, of course, we've been busy with special activities. We've had Christmas parties and visits to Santa. Last weekend we went to the Dickens Fair and saw the gingerbread exhibit at The Embarcadero. You really should go, it's incredible.

MOM: Oh, no we couldn't. We're trying to keep the spiritual significance of Christmas central in our celebration.

MARGE: How boring.

MOM: Not at all. We've got an advent calendar and an advent wreath and we've been to lots of special Christmas programs. We even went to see a living nativity scene in San Ramon. And every night we have a family devotional around our wooden nativity set.

MARGE: *(Sarcastically)* It sounds thrilling.

MOM: Well, you're really missing the meaning of Christmas if you think it's just Santa Claus.

MARGE: You celebrate it your way and I'll celebrate it mine.

MOM: Fine! When you're willing to acknowledge Christmas is a time for real celebration because God sent his Son as a gift to us, let me know.

MARGE: Right.

CHILD: Mom. Mom.

MOM: Just a minute, Marge. Jenny's bugging me again. *(To Jenny)* What?

CHILD: I picked out my story.

MOM: *(Looks at the Bible.)* The Bible?

CHILD: I thought you could read me the Christmas story. After all, it's almost Christmas.

MOM: Don't they read you that at Sunday school?

CHILD: Yeah, but I thought we could read it again.

MOM: No "buts" about it. You've already heard it. Besides I've got to make Jesus' birthday cake tonight. Now go to bed.

CHILD: OK.

MARGE: What were you saying about God's gift?

MOM: Uh, well, listen, like I said, I've got to make Jesus' birthday cake. Bye.

LIGHTS

11
People You'd Never Expect

Topic:
Christmas

Theme:
Many people remember Jesus' birthday, but forget him the rest of the year. They are afraid to let their faith be known. However, if they do, they might be surprised at who else believes in Jesus.

Scripture:
John 1:14; 3:16
Matthew 1:21

Characters:
Person

A Christmas eve service

PERSON: I wasn't really sure I wanted to be here tonight. I just finished my shopping and I've got lots of wrapping to do. And I still have my Christmas cards to send out *(looking at his/her watch)*. Technically they aren't late, at least not for another thirty minutes. So I almost didn't come, but here I am. There's just something about Christmas that makes me come to church.

Celebrating God's gift of His Son seems to help me remember what's really important in my life. I guess once a year is better than not at all.

Business is business and I don't make room for God there. I can't afford to let my business associates think I need anybody, especially not God. They'd think I was crazy.

(Looks out over audience.)

I can't believe it—there's Joe Thompson; he's one of our biggest clients. I didn't know Joe celebrated Jesus' birthday. Then again, maybe his wife made him come. Then again, I spent a lot of years coming here without believing and now I'm here without really doing much about my beliefs during the rest of the year.

Oh, I can't believe it. That couldn't be Fred. *(Peering carefully)* It sure looks like—that's Fred Timber, my neighbor. We haven't spoken to each other since our dog ate their flowers and ruined their lawn. I never would have imagined us both being here.

I guess God does love us all. And He must love us as we are, and not as we should be because I'm sure not as I should be. In fact, I think right after the service I'd better find an all- night nursery. I've got to get some plants for Fred.

LIGHTS

12
More Than A Baby

Topic:
Christmas

Theme:
Jesus' birth is an event that demonstrates God's love for us. But his birth is just the beginning of the relationship he desires to have with us every day of our lives.

Scripture:
John 3:16,17
1 John 4:9

Characters:
Ethel
Lucy

Props:
Santa Claus hat
boxes
two pieces of nativity set (Jesus and Mary)

Two friends are putting ornaments on a Christmas tree.

ETHEL: *(Putting on Santa hat and trying to imitate Santa)* Ho! Ho! Ho! Merry Christmas! What do you think? Did I sound like Santa?

LUCY: No. I think you should stop fooling around and help me finish getting these decorations up. We've got five more boxes to do.

ETHEL: You sure have a lot of Christmas decorations.

LUCY: *(As she is unwrapping an ornament)* Well, I *love* Christmas. All the shopping, and baking, and decorating. Oh, look, this is the first ornament Ted and I had. I'll never forget that Christmas. We bought the biggest tree we could afford and forgot all about the fact that we'd need ornaments. We only had enough money to buy one. This one was it.

ETHEL: That tree must have looked pretty silly.

LUCY: Not to us. It was very special. We had that one ornament, the tree, and then a nativity set my grandmother had given us. I wonder whatever happened to that.

ETHEL: *(Unwrapping a part of the nativity set)* Look, I think I found it. Here's Mary. And here's the baby Jesus. Isn't he cute?

LUCY: Cute?

ETHEL: I've always thought that the baby Jesus looked adorable in the manger in all that hay. I think George and I should get one of these sets. It's so sweet looking, don't you think?

LUCY: Actually, no. I mean yes. Oh, I don't know. It's just that Jesus used to mean so much more to us than a baby in a cradle. I mean *he* used to be the reason we celebrated Christmas. We'd even have a birthday cake for him.

ETHEL: Well, I'm certainly glad you're not a religious fanatic anymore. You've come to your senses and realized that Christmas *is* a time for shopping, and decorating, and baking, and being with family. You're just like everybody else.

LUCY: Being like everybody else seemed to be so important. Ted and I thought that we needed to get ahead, and to do that we left that baby and all that He means behind. We lost sight of the real reason for Christmas.

ETHEL: But you *are* ahead. You've got everything money can buy.

LUCY: And nothing it can't.

ETHEL: What are you talking about?

LUCY: Jesus isn't just a baby. He is God. And that should mean something. *(Pause). I've forgotten how much it means to me.*

ETHEL: I don't get it.

LUCY: Well, let me try to explain it to you.

LIGHTS

13
Salespitch

Topic:
Church

Theme:
A unique approach to presenting the opportunities the church offers would get more people interested in being involved.

Scripture:
Hebrews 10:23-25
Acts 2:44-47
Matthew 5:13

Characters:
Pushy (genuinely enthusiastic)
Passerby (lost and hoping Pushy can give directions)

PUSHY: *(Enthusiastic, has just finished reading material on the worthiness of the church and is eager to share.)* Boy, am I excited, I can't wait to share this. I mean who wouldn't want to get involved? It's fantastic, incredible...*(stops suddenly)*...but I've got to have a creative approach. Hmm. *(Paces a few steps; stops.)* I've got it.

PASSERBY: Could you help me? I'm looking for—

PUSHY: You need my help? That's fantastic. It's wonderful. I know how to help you. I bet you're looking for something to give your life meaning and purpose and I know just the thing.

PASSERBY: I don't think you understand. I'm lost.

PUSHY: You're lost. Of course you're lost. That's great; now you'll be found. You can get involved with people and involved in helping people too.

PASSERBY: But all I need is directions to—

PUSHY: *This* will give you direction. It'll affect every area of your life. You'll find it's worth giving your time, talent, and money to.

PASSERBY: I still don't think you understand.

PUSHY: And the leader of the group is great. He's available twenty-four hours a day to listen to whatever problems or questions you might have.

PASSERBY: *(A little annoyed)* Look, this all sounds very interesting, but what I need to know—

PUSHY: I'm glad you find it interesting because there's more. There's feeding the hungry and helping the poor, and teaching people like you and me how to deal with worry, inflation, and the problems of life.

PASSERBY: It sounds really great, but I need to know how to get to Washington Street.

PUSHY: *(Disappointed)* Oh. *(Pointing toward audience)* Go straight two blocks, and then make a left.

PASSERBY: Thanks. *(Starts to walk away, then stops.)* So what exactly have you been talking about?

PUSHY: The church. It really is worthwhile.

PASSERBY: Well, you've got two blocks to convince me.

(They begin to walk off together.)

PUSHY: There's a tremendous life insurance policy. You'll never have to...

LIGHTS

14
The Earth-ian Way

Topic:
Church As A Body

Theme:
Being a part of the body of Christ means that we must live a lifestyle contrary to the world's way. Scripture makes it clear that we belong to each other, that we need each other, that we are all of equal importance, and that we should develop equal concern for one another.

Scripture:
1 Corinthians 12:12-26
1 John 2:15,16

Characters:
Three aliens

Props:
antennae for aliens
dollar bill

Two aliens are waiting to be beamed up to their ship after observing Earth. They are also waiting for their other crew member to arrive.

FIRST ALIEN: I wonder where she is. She knows we're being beamed up in three-and-a-half minutes.

SECOND ALIEN: She'll be here. Don't worry. I know she wouldn't want to be stuck here on Earth. It has been my least favorite planet to visit.

FIRST ALIEN: The Earth-ians are the most self-centered creatures I have had the displeasure to observe. They are constantly trying to prove that they are better than their neighbors.

SECOND ALIEN: *(Pulling dollar bill out of pocket)* Or that they can possess more of these little green monetary units than their neighbor.

FIRST ALIEN: It's hard to understand why some of them have extremely large shelters while others sleep in doorways and on streets.

SECOND ALIEN: And some of them eat all day long while others don't eat at all. I do not understand their unwillingness to share.

(Third Alien enters.)

FIRST ALIEN: Where have you been? We're due to beam up in two minutes.

THIRD ALIEN: I know. But I observed a group of Earth-ians whose behavior was different from any we've observed. They are called Christ-ians, and they do not abide by the Earth-ian's self-centered system. Instead, they emulate their creator.

SECOND ALIEN: And how is their behavior deviant from the Earth- ians?

THIRD ALIEN: They care for one another. Rather than living independently, they live dependent on one another. When someone has a need, they work together to meet it. They share their food, clothing, even precious green monetary units.

FIRST ALIEN: So they do not live like the Earth-ians?

THIRD ALIEN: They cannot. The Earth-ian way and the Christ-ian way cannot co-exist together in one life.

SECOND ALIEN: Are there many of these Christ-ians?

THIRD ALIEN: Their numbers are increasing.

FIRST ALIEN: *(Standing)* We must be going. But perhaps Earth will be more pleasant the next time we visit, if these Christ-ians can influence the Earth-ians.

LIGHTS

15
Eye'm More Important!

Topic:
Church As A Body

Theme:
No matter what our role is in ministry, it is important. We all need one another. The church needs every Christian to use their gifts if it is to function efficiently and effectively.

Scripture:
Romans 12:4-16
1 Corinthians 12
Ephesians 4

Characters:
Eye
Ear
Foot
Big Toe

Four people enter, representing four body parts: Eye, Ear, Foot, and Big Toe. All try to be first.

EYE: I should go first. After all, without me you couldn't see a thing.

EAR: But without an ear, you couldn't hear anything.

FOOT: But without feet you couldn't have gotten here, so I should go first.

BIG TOE: Why do you guys always have to argue about everything?

EYE: *(Stepping in front of others to microphone)* I am the eye, the most important part of the body. I see the needs. I—

EAR: Now, wait a minute. That's not true.

EYE: Yes, it is. Without me you couldn't do anything. You couldn't help anybody because you couldn't see anybody, much less their needs.

EAR: *(Pushing Eye aside)* But there are some needs you can't see. There are some needs you just hear about. So I am just as important as you are.

FOOT: *(Pushing way to front)* You are forgetting that without me you couldn't get to the needs. I'm your wheels. That makes me, the foot, the most important.

BIG TOE: I don't even care who goes first. The important thing is that we tell these people what it means to be a body.

EYE, EAR, and FOOT: Then I'll go first.

BIG TOE: *(Frustrated)* Then I'll leave. *(Starts to leave; Foot grabs Big Toe.)*

FOOT: You can't leave.

BIG TOE: I'm tired of listening to you all argue.

EYE: Let him go. After all, *he's* only a big toe.

EAR: Yeah, who needs him anyway?

FOOT: We do!

EAR: *(Skeptical)* We do?

FOOT: We can't get very far without him.

EYE: We've still got you.

FOOT: We need him too. Without him I'll be out of balance. We'll have a hard time getting anywhere.

BIG TOE: Really? You need me? *(Looks surprised; says next line more to himself than to audience.)* I didn't know that.

EYE: I hate to say this, but I think maybe we all do need each other.

EAR: If I hear what you're saying, we're all important. *(Looks back at eye, shocked.)* Did I really hear you say that?

EYE: *(Also a little surprised)* Yes, I think I did.

BIG TOE: Then I guess we'd better all leave together.

FOOT: Yes, after all, we do need each other.

EYE: "Eye'll" lead the way.

LIGHTS

16
M.A.S.H.

Topic:
Church's Role

Theme:
The church should be a place for Christians to be refreshed and renewed for their ministry in the world.

Scripture:
Hebrews 10:23-25

Characters:
Announcer
Jami (medic)
John (medic)
First Patient
Second Patient
Third Patient

Props:
medical bag
clipboard

A M.A.S.H. unit. (This is a bit melodramatic, so you can ham it up a little.)

ANNOUNCER: *(Dramatically)* Millions of Christians

throughout the United States and throughout the world are realizing that they are in *enemy* territory. They are being wounded by enemy fire: hatred, prejudice, dishonesty, and other forms of malice. Where do the wounded go? They go to M.A.S.H. units everywhere. There they are healed and then sent back to the battlefield. Let's visit one of the M.A.S.H. units now.

(Jami and John are in charge of the M.A.S.H. unit. Each is talking to a patient. Jami and First Patient are center stage. John and Second Patient are in darkness stage left. Jami and First Patient begin.)

JAMI: What is your problem?

FIRST PATIENT: *(Sitting up)* I've got this incredible headache. I've had it for a week and nothing I do for it helps. I've tried Anacin, aspirin, Excedrin, Tylenol, Empirin—nothing works! *(Feeling sorry for herself, lies down.)*

JAMI: I'm sure we'll be able to help you. *(Helps her up.)*

FIRST PATIENT: Good, because I've had a bad week. My boss told me that if I make one more mistake, I'd be filing for unemployment; my husband is mad at me; my dog flunked out of obedience school, and the IRS wants to audit my last five years of tax returns.

JAMI: You need a good dose of encouragement. Life in enemy territory always causes a need for that. Remember to spend regular time with other Christians in fellowship. Encourage others and you'll find that you'll be encouraged, too!

(Dialogue switches over to John and Second Patient.)

JOHN: Where's the pain?

SECOND PATIENT: Everywhere. I'm achy *everywhere.* And I'm tired. Tired of people calling me stupid. Stupid for being a vegetarian, stupid for majoring in Romantic Literature, and stupid for being a Christian. I'm tired of people telling me what they think I ought to do and why they think I shouldn't be doing what I am.

JOHN: Sounds like you've had a lot of people judging you.

SECOND PATIENT2: Exactly.

JOHN: *(Writing on clipboard)* Diagnosis: A severe case of overjudgment.

SECOND PATIENT: Is there any hope?

JOHN: Sure. There's only one Judge here. Listening to Him and attending fellowship regularly, combined with daily treatments in God's Word, will cure you in no time.

JAMI: *(Calling to John)* John, this one is serious. Can you give me a hand?

JOHN: Sure.

JAMI: I think it's his heart.

JOHN: Where is the pain?

THIRD PATIENT: *(Pointing to heart)* Right here.

JOHN: It's his heart.

JAMI: When did the pain start?

THIRD PATIENT: Well, my girlfriend broke up with me after I got her a job with my uncle's company. My sister took me out to lunch to see if she could borrow five hundred dollars and my car, and when she brought the car back it had some unauthorized body work done. I got a letter from the union and they're increasing my dues, and they don't do beans for me, and then I opened my PG&E bill, and I started thinking about all of that and the pain began.

JAMI: Do you feel like people are taking advantage of you?

THIRD PATIENT: Yes, and I'm tired of being used.

JAMI: You need unconditional love.

JOHN: It's a battlefield out there.

JAMI: And that's why we're here. We offer protection for you. Time in our intensive care unit will take care of *your* heart's needs.

ANNOUNCER: Until next time, this is *(fill in name)* at a M.A.S.H. unit in America.

LIGHTS

17
Be All That You Can Be

Topic:
Commitment

Theme:
Following God's directions for life enables each of us to develop fully into the person He intends us to be.

Scripture:
Psalms 37:3-5
 roverbs 16:9

Characters:
Enlistee (looking for meaning and direction for his life. He had intended to join the army and is somewhat surprised when he discovers what office he is in.)
Recruiter

A heavenly Recruiter is seated behind desk, whistling "Be all that you can be." Enlistee enters, looking a bit lost.

ENLISTEE: Excuse me, but I've noticed some advertisements about being all that you can be and I was wondering if you could help me. I'd really like to be somebody.

RECRUITER: *(Stands and shakes enlistee's hand)* Great. You've come to the right place. Our business is helping people become all that they can.

ENLISTEE: But I'm not sure that you can help *me*.

RECRUITER: Of course we can. We can help everyone who enlists.

ENLISTEE: But I don't think you understand. I don't have any special talents or skills. I can't program a computer or sing or do anything special.

RECRUITER: That doesn't matter. We're helping all kinds of people, from university professors to kindergartners.

ENLISTEE: *(Pauses; thinks a second.)* Boy, you start them young.

RECRUITER: We like to.

ENLISTEE: *(Thinks another second.)* So, you're saying you can take an average guy like me and make him into somebody special.

RECRUITER: Exactly.

ENLISTEE: Well, how long does it take?

RECRUITER: Your whole life.

ENLISTEE: *(Thinking he's kidding)* No, really, be serious.

RECRUITER: I am being serious.

ENLISTEE: But I thought the army had short-term enlistments.

RECRUITER: They do.

ENLISTEE: *(Thinks a second.)* You mean this isn't the army?

RECRUITER: They're two doors down.

ENLISTEE: Oh. *(Thinks.)* So, here I've got to sign up for life to be all that I can be.

RECRUITER: Exactly.

ENLISTEE: *(A little confused)* I knew I needed help and that it would take time, but I didn't know it would take my whole life.

RECRUITER: It's not just you, it's the same for everybody.

ENLISTEE: You mean it takes everybody their whole life to be all that they can be, even the kindergartners?

RECRUITER: Yes.

ENLISTEE: It is interesting, but I need to know more.

RECRUITER: *(Handing him a Bible)* Here's our manual. Would you like to look at it?

ENLISTEE: The Bible?

RECRUITER: That's right.

ENLISTEE: You mean you're recruiting for...for...*(looking up)*...Him?

RECRUITER: Yes, are you still interested?

ENLISTEE: Why don't you tell me more?

RECRUITER: OK. Have a seat.

LIGHTS

18
I Just Want to Talk

Topic:
Communication

Theme:
Communicating with children, especially teenagers, isn't easy. It takes time, self-sacrifice, and constant effort.

Scripture:
Genesis 25:21-26

Characters:
Mom
Cathy (her 16-year-old daughter)

Mom is engrossed in her favorite TV soap opera.

CATHY: *(Entering)* Mom, Mom, you'll never believe what happened today. I am so psyched.

MOM: *(Staring at TV)* Help yourself to a cookie, dear.

CATHY: I don't want a cookie, Mom. Franklin Pierce, the coolest guy in the whole school asked me—

MOM: That's nice, dear.

CATHY: Nice! Mom, he's the coolest guy in the whole school and he wants to take me.

MOM: *(Irritated)* Shhhhh. I'm watching TV.

CATHY: But, Mom.

MOM: Later.

CATHY: *(Disappointed and hurt)* Right. *(Exits left.)*

MOM: *(Turning off TV)* I cannot believe those parents. It's no wonder that family has so many problems. They are always so preoccupied with themselves. Which reminds me. Cathy!

CATHY: What?

MOM: Come here.

CATHY: *(Obviously irritated)* What do you want?

MOM: I just want to talk. How was your day?

CATHY: *(Unenthusiastically)* Great.

MOM: What'd you do?

CATHY: Nothing.

MOM: Well, did you learn anything?

CATHY: No.

MOM: Cathy, I'm trying to talk to you.

CATHY: Right.

MOM: Well, is there anything I can do for you?

CATHY: Can I borrow the car?

MOM: OK.

CATHY: Thanks mom. *(Exits.)*

MOM: Kids today are sure hard to talk to.

LIGHTS

19
The Mall

Topic:
Communication

Theme:
Many people do not know how to listen. They either make the mistake of thinking about what they are going to say while the other person is talking, or they just don't pay attention. We cannot truly communicate unless we learn to listen.

Scripture:
James 3:2-10

Characters:
Two good friends:
   Marge (has forgotten how to listen)
   Susan (is willing to confront her)

A shopping mall

MARGE: Susan, hi, how are you?

SUSAN: Terrible. You'll never believe what happened.

MARGE: That's great.

SUSAN: Great? No, it's not.

MARGE: You know, I'm glad we ran into each other. I've been meaning to call you to ask you and Fred over for dinner.

SUSAN: What I'm trying to tell you is that Fred and I are having—

MARGE: That's perfect. Then we'll see you both on Friday. How about seven? It has been such a long time. I really miss—

SUSAN: Marge, you're not listening.

MARGE: Of course I'm listening. You and Fred are coming over Friday at 7:00.

SUSAN: No, we're not.

MARGE: OK, 7:30. See you then.

SUSAN: Marge, wait.

MARGE: What?

SUSAN: Fred and I are having some problems and I don't think it would be good—

MARGE: Oh, well, in that case never mind. I'll call you soon. Bye.

SUSAN: Marge!

MARGE: What?

SUSAN: What's the matter with you?

MARGE: Nothing. Why do you ask? You're the one who's getting a divorce.

SUSAN: I didn't say I was getting a divorce. I said that Fred and I were having some trouble, and that's no reason for you to be rude.

MARGE: What do you mean?

SUSAN: You aren't listening to me.

MARGE: Yes, I am. Fred's having an affair and you're getting a divorce. Now I really have to be going.

SUSAN: Marge, you aren't listening at all. You are looking around and talking about what *you* want. You are so busy thinking about what you are going to say that you don't hear anything I'm saying.

MARGE: I am not!

SUSAN: Marge!

MARGE: OK, maybe I *was.*

SUSAN: I think you've forgotten how to listen. Sit down and I'll help you learn.

MARGE: But I've really got to get going. I've got a million—

SUSAN: Sit down!

LIGHTS

20
The Waiting Room

Topic:
Counseling

Theme:
Sometimes an objective opinion can help us deal with our problems. Seeking counsel is not something to be ashamed of.

Scripture:
Galatians 6:2
Romans 15:1

Characters:
First Person (counselor)
Second Person (patient)

Props:
sunglasses
magazine

Two people are sitting in a waiting room.

FIRST PERSON: Hi.

SECOND PERSON: Hello.

FIRST PERSON: Waiting?

SECOND PERSON: Uh-huh.

FIRST PERSON: Me too! Why are you wearing those sunglasses? *(Thumbs through magazines; a few nervous seconds pass.)*

SECOND PERSON: I don't want anyone to recognize me.

FIRST PERSON: Oh, I see. Are you nervous?

SECOND PERSON: Uh-huh.

FIRST PERSON: Me too!

SECOND PERSON: *(Takes off sunglasses)* But you look so calm, so relaxed.

FIRST PERSON: You know what they say: appearances can be deceiving. I may look cool, but I don't feel it.

SECOND PERSON: I've never been to a counselor before. I don't know if I really want to talk to one. Is it easy to do?

FIRST PERSON: I don't know. This is my first time, too.

SECOND PERSON: Really? I thought you were probably a salesperson or a teacher. You look so confident. You just don't look like the sort of person that'd have any problems.

FIRST PERSON: Everybody has problems.

SECOND PERSON: You think so?

FIRST PERSON: Yep.

SECOND PERSON: But not everybody goes to a counselor.

FIRST PERSON: No, but you'd be surprised how many people do. All kinds of people too: lawyers, doctors, artists, actors, students. Why, in the last year, the counselors here have seen over one thousand people.

SECOND PERSON: You seem to know a lot about it.

FIRST PERSON: I've looked into it a little.

SECOND PERSON: So you think it's OK to go to a counselor?

FIRST PERSON: Sure!

SECOND PERSON: But don't you feel stupid not being able to solve your own problems?

FIRST PERSON: I kind of look at it differently. I mean at least we're smart enough to get help when we need it. We just need somebody objective to talk to.

SECOND PERSON: But don't you think that all those counselors get together on their coffee breaks and talk about us crazies? They probably compare crazy stories.

FIRST PERSON: I don't think so. I'm sure they keep things confidential. They've got things they'd rather talk about like sports or food. You know how people love to talk about food. Like last night we went to this Chinese restaurant. The food was— *(Realizing the point has just been proven)* Sorry.

SECOND PERSON: So who are you going to talk with today?

FIRST PERSON: You.

SECOND PERSON: Me? What do you mean?

FIRST PERSON: I'm a counselor here.

SECOND PERSON: But you said—

FIRST PERSON: I said I was nervous, and that it was my first time. That's the truth.

SECOND PERSON: You're *nothing* like I expected. You're so easy to talk to.

FIRST PERSON: Want to come in the office and have some coffee? I think we're off to a good start.

SECOND PERSON: Sure.

LIGHTS

21
Playing House

Topic:
Divorce

Theme:
Although there are biblical grounds for divorce, God hates it. He hates it because He loves people and divorce hurts people. Unfortunately, we are teaching our children an unhealthy and unscriptural view of divorce.

Scripture:
Matthew 19:9
1 Corinthians 7:2
2 Corinthians 5:17
Malachi 2:16

Characters:
Three eight-year-old children: Sue, Mary, and Jim

Props:
tie
briefcase
apron

The three children are playing house.

SUE: What do you want to do?

MARY: I don't know. *(To Jim)* What do you want to do?

JIM: I don't know.

SUE: Let's play house.

MARY: OK. I'll be the mommy.

JIM: I'll be the daddy. *(To Sue)* You be the kid.

SUE: I don't want to be the kid.

JIM: OK, I'll be the kid and you be the daddy.

SUE: OK.

(They put on assorted props: tie, apron, etc.)

SUE: Hi, honey, I'm home.

MARY: Hi, darling.

JIM: Hi, dad.

SUE: What's for dinner?

MARY: Spaghetti.

SUE: Spaghetti? You know I hate spaghetti.

MARY: That's what we're having.

SUE: Why'd you cook something I hate?

JIM: I like it!

SUE: Shut up!

MARY: Don't talk to him like that!

SUE: Well, I hate spaghetti.

MARY: It's the only thing I know how to make.

SUE: I'm not eating it.

MARY: Then I'm not going to be the mommy anymore.

SUE: You have to. We're married.

MARY: Then we'll get a divorce.

JIM: You can't. I want a mommy and a daddy.

MARY: You can still have a mommy and a daddy. We just won't live together. It's no big deal. It doesn't even hurt.

JIM: I don't want to play anymore.

SUE: What's the matter?

JIM: It does too hurt.

SUE: What does?

JIM: Divorce. You said it doesn't, but it does.

MARY: We're just pretending.

JIM: I don't want to pretend. I'm not going to get divorced, not ever.

MARY: But everybody does. My mom did.

JIM: So did mine, but I don't think everybody should.

MARY: Well, my mom should have. My dad went out with other women.

JIM: My mom shouldn't have. She just got bored with my dad. She said she didn't love him anymore. How can you just stop loving someone?

SUE: I don't know.

JIM: *(To Sue)* How come your parents aren't divorced?

SUE: I don't know. They fight. I think that they are just too stubborn to give up on each other. I think God helps them.

JIM: Well, when I grow up, I'm going to be just as stubborn and let God help me, too.

LIGHTS

22
You're Not So Bad, After All

Topic:
Exhortation

Theme:
God's people need to be encouragers.

Scripture:
1 Thessalonians 5:11
Hebrews 3:13
Ephesians 4:29

Characters:
Woman
Man

Props:
magazines

A psychiatrist's office. Man sits waiting, nervously. Woman enters. As she does, Man grabs a magazine and begins reading. He covers his face with the magazine, hoping he won't be noticed. However, she notices.

WOMAN: Hi. *(No response.)* Hello?

MAN: *(From behind magazine)* Hello.

WOMAN: *(Referring to magazine)* Wouldn't you do better if you turned that right-side up? I imagine it'd kind of hard reading it upside down.

MAN: *(Embarrassed, turns magazine around)* I was just looking at the pictures anyway. *(Goes back to reading.)*

WOMAN: Is there a copy of *Working Woman*?

MAN: *(Looking at the pile)* Yes, here you go.

WOMAN: Oh rats. This is last month's. I've already read it.

MAN: I couldn't care less.

WOMAN: Sorry, I was just trying to be friendly—you know, strike up a conversation? *(Realizing he's not interested, she begins reading magazine. A few seconds of uneasiness pass.)*

MAN: What did you mean you were just trying to be friendly? Are you trying to pick me up, because I'm really—

WOMAN: I wasn't trying to pick you up. I was just trying to be friendly. Besides, you're not even my type.

MAN: Oh. *(Pause.)* What do you mean, I'm not your type?

Aren't I macho enough? Don't I wear the right after-shave? I know I put deodorant on. Is it my clothes? These are my work clothes. Wh—?

WOMAN: No, really, it's not any of those things. You're just not my type.

MAN: Good, because you certainly aren't mine.

WOMAN: So what kind of an office is this? *(She knows full well what kind of an office it is.)*

MAN: It's, uh, it's a dentist's office.

WOMAN: No, it isn't. It's a psychiatrist's office.

MAN: Well, why'd you ask?

WOMAN: I wanted to see if you are as insecure as you look.

MAN: What's that supposed to mean?

WOMAN: It's just that you're the perfect picture of in-security. Obviously you've never been to a shrink before.

MAN: He's not a shrink. He's a psychiatrist, and there's nothing wrong with going to see one.

WOMAN: I know. I'm going to him, too.

MAN: You are?

WOMAN: This is my first time.

MAN: But you don't act sick, and you look...*(looks her over)*...you look great.

WOMAN: Well, aside from looking a little insecure, you're not too bad yourself.

MAN: Really? You mean I'm really not too bad? Nobody has ever said that about me before. Wow!

(They are a little embarrassed by their openness. They look back at the magazines.)

MAN: You know, I feel great. I'm not so bad. You're a terrific person.

WOMAN: No, I'm not.

MAN: Yes, you are. Boy, oh, boy, I'm not so bad. *(Gets up.)* Hey, I'm not going to visit with the shrink today. I feel great. How about some lunch?

WOMAN: OK. After all, who needs a psychiatrist? I'm a terrific person.

MAN: Yeah, and I'm not so bad.

LIGHTS

23
The Dump

Topic:
Eternal security

Theme:
Eternal security is not guaranteed by anything people do.
Once people accept Jesus Christ as Lord and Savior, they
will always be children of God.

Scripture:
Ephesians 2:8-10
John 6:39,40
Romans 8:16,17

Characters:
Jami (upset about her loss)
Carla (Jami's friend)

Props:
garbage bags
brown paper sacks

---

*Two friends are looking through some garbage at the
dump.*

CARLA: I can't believe I actually let you talk me into coming here. We're never going to find it.

JAMI: Don't say that. We've got to find it.

CARLA: But there's garbage dumped everywhere.

JAMI: That's why they call it a dump.

CARLA: It smells so bad.

JAMI: Just be thankful we don't have to look everywhere. The man at the gate said my garbage should be somewhere around here.

CARLA: How could you throw something so important away?

JAMI: My mother did it. She was visiting and to her it looked like an ordinary brown bag.

CARLA: *(Finding a brown bag)* Is this it?

JAMI: *(Grabbing the bag and looking in it)* No, that's not it.

CARLA: *(Looking in another bag)* This definitely isn't it— a moldy, unidentifiable sandwich and a rotten Easter egg.

JAMI: It's got to be here.

CARLA: Before I look any more, I want to know exactly what we're looking for.

JAMI: I told you: my eternal security.

CARLA: What's your life insurance doing in a brown paper bag?

JAMI: It's not just my life insurance. It's my *eternal* security. All my certificates from Bible seminars, the list of Bible studies I've attended, my confessed sins, my certificate of baptism, *everything* is in there.

CARLA: I didn't know a person had to keep all that stuff.

JAMI: I'm keeping it just in case God has second thoughts about letting me in to heaven.

CARLA: *(Holds up another bag)* Is this it?

JAMI: *(Recognizing it)* That's it! *(Hugs Carla.)* You found it. Thank you so much.

CARLA: You're sure that's it? I don't want to have to come back out here again—ever!

JAMI: I'm sure. I've carried that bag around with me for three- and-a-half years. I'd know this bag anywhere.

CARLA: Why don't you look inside, just to be sure.

JAMI: OK. *(Opens bag.)* Oh, no. All my lists and certificates are missing. Everything is gone except this note. *(Looks the note over.)*

CARLA: Are you sure that's the right bag?

JAMI: Of course I'm sure.

CARLA: Well, why don't you read the note?

JAMI:

"Dear Jami:

Remember who saved you. Remember you will always be one of my children. Trust me. You needn't carry that bag with you any longer.

Love, God"

CARLA: Wow! God wrote you a note. I've always wanted to get a special message from Him. Boy, are you lucky. God must really love you!

JAMI: I guess I don't need this bag after all. *(Tosses the bag.)* I'm sorry I made you come out here and look through all this garbage. I really did think my eternal security was in that bag. Now I know He's got it.

CARLA: Oh, well, it's not every day you spend with a friend at the dump. But, if you don't mind, I'd really like to get out of here. I need a shower, and to be perfectly honest, you do, too.

JAMI: Let's go.

LIGHTS

24
The Simple Way to Fish

Topic:
Evangelism

Theme:
Witnessing is telling others about Jesus and what He has done in our lives.

Scripture:
John 4:26-42

Characters:
Harold
Victoria

Husband and wife are talking at the end of the day.

VICTORIA: You'll never guess who became a Christian.

HAROLD: Who?

VICTORIA: George Jenkins.

HAROLD: That's impossible. I've been sharing with him for years. He's not even close.

VICTORIA: He accepted Jesus Christ as his Lord and Savior.

HAROLD: Are you sure?

VICTORIA: Yes.

HAROLD: *(Upset)* How could you do that to me?

VICTORIA: Do what?

HAROLD: Lead him to Christ.

VICTORIA: I thought that's what we are supposed to do.

HAROLD: *(Pouting)* But he's *my* friend.

VICTORIA: Then be happy.

HAROLD: *(Unenthusiastically)* I am. But it's not fair. I've tried everything. He should have become a Christian with me. I tried the gentle approach. I told him how meaningless life was without Jesus, and how he'd never find real happiness unless he accepted Christ into his life.

VICTORIA: *(A little sarcastic)* Oh, that's real gentle. What'd you do next?

HAROLD: Then I got kind of tough and told him how he shouldn't be using cocaine or be drinking as much as he does, and how he shouldn't cheat on his taxes or he'd wind up in hell.

VICTORIA: Oh.

HAROLD: What did *you* do?

VICTORIA: I just told him how Jesus has changed my life. I told him what it was like before and what it's like now.

HAROLD: What else?

VICTORIA: Well, I told him what Jesus did on the cross and why he did it.

HAROLD: And he believed you?

VICTORIA: Why wouldn't he? It's the truth.

HAROLD: Well, I don't want you talking to Fred Johnson until I've had a chance.

VICTORIA: Why?

HAROLD: I think I know what I've been doing wrong now. I can't wait to tell him what Jesus has done for me.

LIGHTS

25
The Vowels

Topic:
Evil

Theme:
Why is there evil in the world? No one knows exactly. However, it is obvious God allows it, identifies with it, uses it, and will ultimately overcome it.

Scripture:
2 Corinthians 5:21
Ephesians 5:15,16
1 John 2:13

Characters:
The vowels: A, E, I, O, U, and Y

Props:
large cardboard letters for each of the vowels

Six people enter, each carrying a letter.

A: We are vowels.

Y: Now you may ask, "Y" are we here?

I: We are here to tell you a little about...

E: ...Evil, me.

Y: "Y" is there evil, and "Y" does God...

A: ...Allow it? We know He does. Evil is everywhere. Look at Job. God allowed Satan to do terrible things to him. And evil can happen to anyone.

E: Talk to your friends, or look at the front page in your newspaper. I am everywhere.

U: God Uses evil, too! Because of the evil that happened to Jesus, everyone has the opportunity to know God and to live with Him forever.

I: That's why God can Identify with evil. Jesus was dealt with evilly. He was crucified unjustly. He knows what evil is like, and he knows what it is like to be affected by it.

O: And "O" is for God Overcoming evil.

E: What do you mean?

O: Jesus' resurrection will ultimately put an end to all evil.

E: I don't think I like the direction this conversation is taking.

O: It's true. In the end you'll be extinct, crushed, gone forever.

E: *(Protesting)* But that's not fair. I don't want to be extinct. I'm having too much fun.

O: *(Adamant)* God *will* overcome evil.

A: That's all we really have to say. "A" is for God allowing evil.

E: "E" is for evil, me, however long I may last. *(Sniffles)*.

I: "I" is for God identifying with evil.

O: *(Looking at E)* "O" is for God overcoming evil.

U: And "U" is for God using evil.

Y: And "Y," "Y" is there evil? Well, we're not exactly sure, but since you have to live with it, we thought we might help you understand it.

LIGHTS

26
The Zoo

Topic:
Evolution/Creation

Theme:
There are many cracks in the facts of evolution. Looking at the facts, it is sometimes easier to believe creation than evolution.

Scripture:
Genesis 1,2
Job 38

Characters:
Mom (sophisticated, trying to share her wisdom with her daughter)
Suzy (precocious eight-year-old daughter)

Mom and Suzy are at the zoo.

MOM: Now, darling, I want you to look at these monkeys carefully. These are your oldest ancestors.

SUZY: Really?

MOM: That's correct. Of course these aren't the actual monkeys, but they probably looked a great deal like these gibbons.

SUZY: Why don't they look more like us?

MOM: Because of the process called evolution by natural selection. You see, honey, all life started from a single cell that mutated hundreds of thousands of times until it became a monkey.

SUZY: And what about zebras, elephants, giraffes, and kangaroos? Did they all come from that first cell?

MOM: That's right, honey. Of course, the cell had to mutate differently.

SUZY: Well, where did that first cell come from?

MOM: *(She was not prepared for that question, but she does not want to show any hint of ignorance.)* Another way we know these monkeys are our ancestors is through the discovery of fossils.

SUZY: You mean old bones?

MOM: That's right. Scientists discovered bones from monkeys who lived thousands of years ago.

SUZY: Have they found fossils that show the monkeys developed into people?

MOM: Well, no, not exactly, but I'm sure they will. Scientists do have portions of a few of our ancestors. One of them is called Piltdown man.

SUZY: But mom, they told us in school that Piltdown man was an artificially aged human skull.

MOM: How can you remember that when you can't remember to pick up your socks?

SUZY: I just thought it was interesting.

MOM: *(Changing the subject)* Let's go look at the hippos.

SUZY: But mommy, when are these monkeys going to evolve into people?

MOM: I don't know, honey. Let's go look at the hippos.

SUZY: But mom...

MOM: What?

SUZY: Do these monkeys think and feel like us? Do they have a personality?

MOM: I don't know. Let's go look—

SUZY: But mom...

MOM: What?

SUZY: How did that one cell manage to make everything in the world?

MOM: I don't know. Why don't you ask your daddy when we get home?

SUZY: OK.

LIGHTS

27
Friendship Recovery

Topic:
Friendship

Theme:
Being friends requires being unselfish and understanding, even when we're tired of being unselfish and understanding. Sometimes it means making an extra effort, going an "extra mile," just to let the other person know you really care.

Scripture:
Proverbs 17:7
1 Peter 4:8
1 John 4:7

Characters:
Mary
Jane

Two people are on stage: Mary is stage left; Jane is stage right. They are obviously in a fight.

MARY: Why should I care if she cares anyway? *(Looks stage right at Jane.)* I mean you win some, you lose some, right? I mean friendship is supposed to give and take. And all she's been doing is taking. I mean, I shouldn't have to put up with this, right? I mean, no friend should, right? *(Turns again to Jane.)* I don't care that you don't care. *(Turns and faces stage left.)*

JANE: Who wants a friendship where the other person gets tired of caring, anyway? Can you believe that? She's tired of caring? Well, I'm tired, too. I'm tired of telling her my problems. *(Looks over at Mary.)* Hear that? I'm tired of telling you my problems. That'll fix her. *(Turns and faces stage right.)*

MARY: *(Looks stage right)* The problem is, I do care that she doesn't care. I don't want to lose our friendship. We've had so many great times, but she's been acting so selfish, you know what I mean? I guess I could try to be more understanding. She has been through a lot. *(Looks over at her.)* But I'm not going to apologize. I mean I haven't done anything wrong. *(Faces stage left.)*

JANE: But I don't want to fix her. What I really want is our friendship back. I suppose she *is* right: I have been talking an awful lot about myself recently. And come to think of it, I haven't really listened much. But what can I do about it? *(Looks over stage left.)* I mean she looks pretty mad. *(Looks up as if listening.)* Apologize? Apologize! How humiliating. *(Looks stage left, then up, then stage left again. Takes a deep breath and starts moving toward Mary. Mary starts moving at the same time).*

BOTH: *(Simultaneously)* Hey, I'm sorry. *(They both look embarrassed, then start again.)* I mean, I've been thinking and— *(They laugh and start again.)* I'm sorry, go ahead.

MARY: No, please, you first. After all, you have been doing most of the talking.

JANE: I know. I'm sorry. I've been really selfish. I don't really have an excuse. I mean, it's just so many things have been going wrong in my life, I haven't given much thought to you or anyone else. Will you forgive me?

MARY: Sure. I think I'm at fault, too. I should have been more understanding.

JANE: Friends?

MARY: Friends.

(They begin to shake hands, then hug.)

LIGHTS

28
The Meeting

Topic:
Friendship

Theme:
Expectations come with friendship. These expectations must be understood by all parties in a relationship. Any misunderstandings about these expectations must be openly discussed if reconciliation is to occur.

Scripture:
Mark 19:19
Colossians 3:12-15
Philippians 2:3,4

Characters:
Jami (insecure, hot-headed, jumps to conclusions)
Karen (Jami's friend, never meant to hurt her feelings)

Two good friends have a misunderstanding and subsequent confrontation.

JAMI: *(Upset)* Where were you?

KAREN: Hi, Jami.

JAMI: Don't "Hi, Jami me." Where were you?

KAREN: When?

JAMI: At lunchtime.

KAREN: Eating lunch in the cafeteria.

JAMI: With who?

KAREN: Nancy, the new girl.

JAMI: I knew it. It's always Nancy. Nancy this, Nancy that. You don't care about me anymore.

KAREN: It was *one* lunch.

JAMI: One lunch will turn into two, and two into three, and before you know it, you won't have any time for me. But that's okay. I won't care. Anyway, you are breaking every rule of friendship.

KAREN: I didn't know there were any rules.

JAMI: Of course there are. Friendship is not "Que Sera Sera." There are rules and you are breaking them.

KAREN: You never told me about any rules.

JAMI: The first rule is to be available, which you weren't today.

KAREN: I was working.

JAMI: And eating lunch with Nancy.

KAREN: This is ridiculous.

JAMI: The second rule is to be unselfish, which you aren't.

The third one is to be loyal, and you probably broke that one telling Nancy all my faults, and the fourth one is to be honest, which you aren't, or you'd tell me that our friendship is over.

KAREN: But it isn't.

JAMI: *(Very dramatic)* I don't care anyway. I knew having friends was risky business. I won't care what you do or say. It is finito, *finished*. The final chapter has been written. I'm going to get some new friends, better friends—ones who'll follow all the rules, and I'll tell them what a lousy friend you were, and don't bother trying to call and apologize because I *won't* answer your calls. Good-bye.

KAREN: Wait a minute. Who's breaking the rules now?

JAMI: What rules?

KAREN: The ones you just told me about.

JAMI: *(Thinks a minutes, then smiles.)* Me. I'm sorry. I got a little carried away. Forgive me?

KAREN: Of course.

JAMI: Are you free for dinner?

KAREN: No. I'm having dinner with Nancy.

JAMI: What?

KAREN: I'm just kidding. Shall we have Chinese or pizza?

LIGHTS

29
The Wrong Approach

Topic:
Friendship

Theme:
Friendships would be much easier to maintain if we could just follow a formula for perfect friendships. Unfortunately, it is not that simple, and although rules and guidelines can help, the bottom line is that friendships take time and effort.

Scripture:
Proverbs 17:17
John 15:13
Romans 12:15

Characters:
Nora (friendless)
First Girl
Second Girl

Props:
one small book
magazine

Nora is in the park. Other people are scattered on stage, victims of her friendship attempts.

NORA: Here I am in this beautiful park with nobody to talk to and nothing to do. I guess you could say I'm friendless; I really *don't* have any friends, but I'm working on it. I bought this little book, "How to Have Great Friendships." It says there are five basic steps to making a great friendship, and I'm going to try every one. Step One: Make relationships top priority. I can handle that. Why, I'll just get a telephone answering machine so I'll be available twenty-four hours a day, and I'll schedule a couple of hours daily just to be with my friend—that is, as soon as I get one. Now for Step Two: Work toward transparency. Hmm. I guess that means being completely honest. *(Looks around, sees girl reading magazine stage left)*. Oh, that girl looks like she'd be a good friend. I'll try this one on her. *(Walks over to the girl.)* Excuse me, but I've got to be honest with you, especially if we're going to be good friends. So, let me start by telling you something I've never told anyone before.

FIRST GIRL: But I don't even know y—

NORA: It's really important that we begin our relationship honestly, so I want you to know that I dye my hair. I know that seems like a silly thing to tell you, but I don't want to give you a false impression.

SECOND GIRL: Look, I don't mean to be rude, but I don't know you. I don't know why you're telling me—

NORA: Now as for you, I think your clothes are a *bit* tacky. They're outdated, they lack style, if you know what I mean. You could look a lot better if you—

FIRST GIRL: *(Rising to exit)* You have a lot of nerve. I don't even know you!

NORA: *(Disappointed, but not discouraged)* I must have done something wrong. I guess I should try the next step. *(Looking at book)* Oh, Steps Three and Four seem to go together. Step Three: Verbalize affection; Step Four: Show gestures of love. *(Sees girl crossing stage; stops her.)* My name is Nora *(Shakes hand; keeps hold of it)*.

SECOND GIRL: *(Acting cautious)* Hi.

NORA: I'd really like to be your friend. I think we could have a good friendship.

SECOND GIRL: Yeah, well, maybe. Could you let go of my hand?

NORA: I'm sorry. I was just trying to be friendly. You know, show affection and gestures of love.

SECOND GIRL: Maybe we should get to know a little bit more about each other first. I think you need to know someone before you start showing affection.

NORA: *(Shocked)* Oh, well I've been reading this book and...*(looking in the book)*. Oh, I see where you're at. Step Five: Create space. You need some space. *(Backing off)* That's fine. Maybe we could get together next week, or the week after, or the week after, or the week after.

SECOND GIRL: Or the week after that, or maybe never. *(Exits.)*

NORA: *(Thoughtfully)* I just don't get it. I'm practicing all the steps. Maybe I should start out a little slower. I suppose great friendships aren't made in one afternoon. Maybe I'll have better luck tomorrow. Until then, I'll keep reading.

LIGHTS

30
Adoption Agency

Topic:
God's Adoption

Theme:
God is the creator of all, but Father only to those who choose to accept Jesus Christ as their Lord and Savior. He then adopts us, making us legal heirs of his kingdom.

Scripture:
Ephesians 1:5,6
John 1:10-13
Romans 8:15-17

Characters:
Angel
Person
Tempter

Props:
angel hat
tempter hat
adoption agency sign

Person is sitting at adoption agency desk.

PERSON: This whole thing just doesn't sound right. Are you sure there is no waiting list?

ANGEL: There's no waiting list.

PERSON: But every adoption agency has a waiting list.

ANGEL: We're not like other agencies.

PERSON: And I'll be considered his legitimate child, a legal heir?

ANGEL: That's right.

PERSON: And nothing I've done in my past can be held against me. I mean, He can't change his mind when He learns about some of the things I've done?

ANGEL: Your former life doesn't matter. He completely blots it out. It's as if it never existed.

PERSON: But I'm not good enough for Him to adopt me. I've made too many mistakes. Maybe there's been a computer error. I'm probably not supposed to be here.

ANGEL: *(Interrupting)* There's no mistake. He invited you. Now I'll go tell Him you're here. *(Exits stage right.)*

(Tempter enters stage left.)

TEMPTER: Don't do it. God may be your creator, but you don't have to let Him become your Father. You've already got a family, the family of darkness. You don't want to leave us, do you? Why, we'd be heartbroken!

PERSON: But this is a chance for me to have real meaning in my life.

TEMPTER: Who needs real meaning?

PERSON: I'll be a legitimate heir to his kingdom.

TEMPTER: But you're already a part of a kingdom, the kingdom of darkness.

PERSON: But my life is empty. This adoption into his family offers me all the things I've been looking for.

TEMPTER: *(Trying a different tack)* But what if it's all a scam? What if none of what He's offering is true? What if He doesn't even exist? What if everything you learned about evolution is true, and there is no God, no creator? What if you're just a chance mutation? What if there's no one to adopt you at all?

PERSON: Why would *you* be here then?

TEMPTER: Well, uh, you see, I...

ANGEL: He wants to see you now.

PERSON: Great. *(Walks off stage right.)*

(Angel smiles and waves at Tempter. Tempter stomps off.)

LIGHTS

31
The Ad Campaign

Topic:
God's Character

Theme:
The character of God is often misunderstood. It is difficult for people to understand how God can be so powerful and personal.

Scripture:
Psalms 139
Hebrews 4:13
Matthew 10:29,30

Characters:
First Person
Second Person
Third Person
Fourth Person

Four well-dressed advertising interns are working on their first campaign. They are seated with pencil and paper in hand.

FIRST PERSON: OK. Let's get started. *(Pause.)* Where should we begin?

THIRD PERSON: I think we should probably start with God.

FIRST PERSON: OK. *(Speaking toward sky)* God, we're here on your behalf. You see your image down here isn't quite what it used to be, and we're going to help you get it straightened out. We think if people knew more about you they'd be more interested.

FOURTH PERSON: We're going to do a complete media blitz.

SECOND PERSON: First, we're going to get a slogan like, "Where's The Beef?" and then we're going to plaster it everywhere: billboards, posters, bumper stickers. You know, the works.

FIRST PERSON: We want people to realize you are just like everybody else. I mean, you were a man; you can identify with taxes and inflation. *(Pause, then as if they've got a great idea)* How about this: a billboard with a picture of God in outer space. The slogan would be, "Meet A Man Out Of This World."

(Others give no encouraging response.)

FOURTH PERSON: I don't think so. He did come to earth as a man, but He is God.

SECOND PERSON: I don't think we could get a picture anyway.

THIRD PERSON: I think we should emphasize his friendliness. You know, the idea that God will go with you anywhere, bowling alleys, golf courses, sporting events.

FOURTH PERSON: I don't know.

THIRD PERSON: The slogan could be something like, "With God On Your Side, You'll Always Be A Winner."

(No positive reaction from others.)

FIRST PERSON: *(Shaking head)* But in the most practical sense of the word, that isn't true.

SECOND PERSON: I think it should be on a more conceptual level. Like, "God: He's The Real Thing." It'll make people think.

FOURTH PERSON: But it doesn't *say* anything. I mean, after all, what is the real thing?

SECOND PERSON: *(Without any hesitation)* Coke.

FOURTH PERSON: You see what I mean?

SECOND PERSON: I guess you're right.

FOURTH PERSON: It should be more personal. God *is* our father.

SECOND PERSON: *(Thinking out loud)* OK. How about "Meet *The* Big Daddy?"

FIRST PERSON: That's not very reverent.

FOURTH PERSON: I don't think He'd like it.

SECOND PERSON: It was just an idea.

FIRST PERSON: What we need is something short and explicit expressing God's love, mercy, righteousness, omnipresence, omniscience, and omnipotence.

SECOND PERSON: Sure.

(They pace the floor a few seconds.)

THIRD PERSON: I've got it. "Awesome But Personal."

SECOND PERSON: It's kind of simple, but...

FOURTH PERSON: ...it's accurate.

FIRST PERSON: And it's the best we've come up with. *(Looking skyward)* It may not be as good as, "Where's The Beef?" but at least it's a beginning.

LIGHTS

32
The Elevator

Topic:
God's Character

Theme:
Misconceptions about God's character often keep people from getting to know Him.

Scripture:
Genesis 1:26
Psalms 90:2
Malachi 3:6
Revelation 22:12

Characters:
Sam (views God as a distant entity; suffers from claustrophobia)
Jenny (average committed Christian)
Chris (snob, self-righteous, self-centered, doesn't trust people or God)

Three people are in an elevator when it suddenly stops.

SAM: Oh no. What happened?

JENNY: I don't know.

CHRIS: Obviously, the elevator is stuck.

SAM: *(Begins pacing)* Oh no. I hope they get it fixed soon. I'm very claustrophobic, you know.

CHRIS: I don't know, and I don't care.

JENNY: *(Kindly)* I'll push the emergency button, and I'm sure they'll get it fixed right away.

CHRIS: I doubt it. People are so incompetent nowadays. It'll probably take hours.

SAM: *(Yells)* Help. Somebody help!

JENNY: *(Trying to console Sam)* Just relax. It'll be all right.

CHRIS: You'd think in this modern age they'd be able to keep an elevator running. The world's a disaster. What with crime, bigotry, terrorism, and inflation, it's a wonder we all survive.

JENNY: It's nice to know *I'm* not going to live here forever.

CHRIS: *(Suspiciously)* What do you mean? Where are you going to be?

JENNY: In heaven.

CHRIS: Give me a break.

JENNY: It's true.

CHRIS: Well, I certainly hope you're not going to start telling me how I can get there because I don't want to hear it. I don't even believe in God.

(While Chris and Jenny have been talking, Sam's pacing has increased to a fervor.)

SAM: Help. The walls are closing in. Somebody open up!

JENNY: *(Consoling Sam)* It's all right. I'm sure somebody is fixing the elevator right now.

CHRIS: God is a distant entity who indiscriminately causes pain and suffering to people. We're just toys of his, manipulated, used, and when we are broken, He discards us.

SAM: I thought you said you didn't believe in God.

CHRIS: I don't, but if I did, I know that's what He'd be like.

JENNY: That's *not* what God is like.

CHRIS: *(Sarcastically)* No, I'm sure *your* God is all loving, and kind, and caring.

JENNY: I didn't say that and I wouldn't be telling the truth if I did.

CHRIS: Here comes the lecture.

JENNY: It's not a lecture, but God is much more complex than any of us know. He's just, merciful, unchanging, eternal, powerful, and He cares about people, *all* people.

CHRIS: Come on, don't try to—

SAM: You think He cares about me?

JENNY: I think He even cares that you are feeling claustrophobic.

SAM: *(Coming to his senses)* Oh, that's right. I'd almost forgotten. *(Yelling)* Somebody help!

JENNY: I'm going to pray that these elevator doors open.

SAM: You really think God cares enough about me to make this elevator work?

JENNY: I know He cares about you, but whether He's going to make the elevator work, I don't know. *(Prays silently.)*

CHRIS: Even if it works it will just be a coincidence; that's all it will be, a coincidence.

SAM: It's working. That's incredible. *(To Jenny)* Thank you, thank you.

JENNY: Don't thank me, thank Him.

CHRIS: *(To Jenny)* It was just a coincidence. But I'll thank God I don't have to listen to *you* any more. *(Exits.)*

SAM: *(Timidly)* Well, maybe it is just coincidence, but those doors did open, and if there really is a God who cares about me, I want to know Him. Could you tell me about what God is like?

JENNY: Sure.

LIGHTS

33
The Strike

Topic:
God's Character

Theme:
God is holy, personal, powerful, unchanging, and always here.

Scripture:
Leviticus 11:44
Psalms 99:3
Malachi 3:6
Ephesians 1:18-20

Characters:
Three people on strike
Heavenly Arbitrator

Props:
placards for strike

Outside the Heavenly Arbitrator's office

FIRST PERSON: *(Entering)* He didn't accept our last offer.

SECOND PERSON: I don't think this strike is ever going to end.

THIRD PERSON: I guess we should look at the contract again.

FIRST PERSON: Let's concede "holy."

SECOND PERSON: We already did that.

THIRD PERSON: The Heavenly Arbitrator gave us no choice.

SECOND PERSON: "Holy" was non-negotiable.

FIRST PERSON: It seems like all of these attributes are non-negotiable.

SECOND PERSON: Maybe "here" is negotiable. Maybe we could get Him to limit his presence among us. Like, once every two hundred years or something.

THIRD PERSON: Here comes the Heavenly Arbitrator. Let's see if she thinks He'll concede.

(Heavenly Arbitrator enters.)

SECOND PERSON: You know, we were thinking that we'd be willing to concede "Holy" if He'd accept visitation rights.

HEAVENLY ARBITRATOR: Visitation rights?

SECOND PERSON: Yeah, like He could visit us once every two hundred years.

HEAVENLY ARBITRATOR: I'm sure that would be unacceptable. He's always going to be here.

THIRD PERSON: But it's so intimidating having Him around all the time.

HEAVENLY ARBITRATOR: I'm sorry; He's always everywhere.

FIRST PERSON: Well, if we concede His "presence" and being "Holy," do you think He'd give up some of his power?

HEAVENLY ARBITRATOR: No.

SECOND PERSON: Do you think He'll ever change his mind?

HEAVENLY ARBITRATOR: No. I don't think so. He's always the same.

SECOND PERSON: But it's not fair. He's not giving in on anything. This contract is "as is." There are no exceptions; no amendments.

THIRD PERSON: He won't give up on being holy.

SECOND PERSON: Or being here.

FIRST PERSON: Or any of his power. We might as well just stop these negotiations. We'll never reach a settlement.

HEAVENLY ARBITRATOR: But you're overlooking one thing.

FIRST PERSON: What?

HEAVENLY ARBITRATOR: He's personal. He cares about each of you individually. Remember you're his creation and He wants to be your Father.

SECOND PERSON: Maybe this strike *is* senseless.

THIRD PERSON: We'll probably be here for eternity.

FIRST PERSON: Well, I for one am going to cross the picket line.

SECOND PERSON: Me, too.

LIGHTS

34
World's Greatest Lover

Topic:
God's Love

Theme:
Real love is best exemplified by God giving his Son. In our search for romance we often mistake romance for love. To truly understand love, we must seek to become the best "lovers" we can by following God's example.

Scripture:
John 3:16
1 John 4:7-21
Ephesians 5:1,2

Characters:
Terri

Props:
newspaper

Terri is on stage reading Personals section of newspaper. She is oblivious of audience at first.

TERRI: "Attractive male, mid thirties, loves moonlit nights and walking on the beach is looking for blonde, blue-eyed female who enjoys the same." *(Shakes head no.)* I don't think so. *(Seeing that there are people in auditorium, is a bit embarrassed.)* Oh, you're probably wondering what I'm doing reading the personal ads. I don't want you to think I don't know anything about love, because I do. And it's not that I can't get a date; I can. It's just, well, I'm looking for that perfect someone. I can see right through these advertisements. I won't pick a loser. I won't be blinded by love or one of these ads. I am perfectly aware that it is easier to fall in love than to stay in love. I'll show you what I mean. Listen to this ad: "Male, twenty-five, Rocky look-alike, gentle and caring, seeks to make all of your dreams come true." Fat chance! This guy is too good to be true. He doesn't mention *any* of his faults. Everybody has them. *(Goes back to paper.)*

Oooh, listen to this guy. He thinks I'll call him just because he wears Jovan's Sex Appeal. I know that there are more important things than cologne. I won't call him. *(Thinks a second.)* I've learned a lot of other things, too, like real communication is more important than chatter. I know I need to concentrate on becoming the best lover *I* can be, instead of worrying about finding the best lover. *(Looks back at paper.)*

What's this? "World's Greatest Lover." How can anyone claim to be the World's Greatest Lover? Let me see what else it says. "For God so loved the world that He gave His one and only Son, that whosoever believes in Him shall not perish, but have eternal life." *(Looks up.)*

What does that have to do with being a great lover? *(Reads verse again, this time more slowly.)* "For God so loved the world that He gave his one and only Son, that whosoever believes in Him shall not perish, but have eternal life."

(Thinks a second.) Well, I've heard God *is* love, and this says He showed love by giving us his Son, and giving—that's what love is all about, so I guess God *is* the World's Greatest Lover. *(Pause.)* Anyway, I'm not going to argue with Him about it, are you?

LIGHTS

35
Long Distance

Topic:
God's Plan

Theme:
Having a relationship with God is not as simple as making a phone call once a month. It requires trusting, knowing, following and obeying Him. In other words, allowing Him to be involved with us and our activities on a daily basis.

Scripture:
John 3:13-21

Characters:
Laurie (a self-made, successful business woman)

Props:
phone
buzzer

In a busy office, the manager is aggressively working on the day's activities.

LAURIE: Thanks for the information. That'll help us get a better deal. *(Hangs up the phone.)* Marcee, get Mr. Clog on the phone. We need to convince him to drop his price on those computer parts. Shirley just told me his company is close to bankruptcy. Right. Line 4 is long distance? OK. Charter here. *(Change in tone)* Oh, hi, Lord. I was just about to call you. Yes, I know it's been a while. It's great to talk to you now. *(Buzzer sounds.)* Could you hold a minute? Thanks. *(Tone changes again.)* Charter here. No, absolutely not. I don't care how sick you are, we need you here, now. I don't care if you do have the Taiwan flu. Get yourself here within the hour or get yourself another job. *(Tone changes.)* I'm sorry for the interruption. I was having a little trouble with one of my employees. I'm sure you understand. Yes. One does need a lot of patience. *(Buzzer sounds again.)* Oh dear. Could you hold again? Thanks. *(Tone changes.)* Charter here. Yes, Marcee. No, absolutely not. Tell him that we won't pay it. I don't care if he does lose money on the deal. They're the ones close to bankruptcy. They should be thankful we're paying them anything at all. *(Tone changes.)* Sorry, Lord. *(Buzzer sounds.)* Oh, I've got to put you on hold just one more time. *(Tone changes.)* Charter here. Oh, hi sweetheart. Today is the class play? Oh no, I thought it was tomorrow. I'm sorry, honey, I just can't get away. I know I promised but I just can't. Next time, okay? I'll see you when I get home, honey. I've got to go. I'm on a long-distance call. Lord, I'm sorry for all these interruptions. It's just a very busy time of year. I want you to know I appreciate your patience and understanding. I'm going to keep in touch more this year. Visit? No. No, I wouldn't want to take up your valuable time. You have enough things to do without helping me. I appreciate the offer, but, really I think long-distance is much better than You being here.

LIGHTS

36
The Droid

Topic:
God's Plan

Theme:
God created man in his image, with the purpose of becoming like Him.

Scripture:
Romans 8:29
Genesis 1:26
Psalms 8:4,5

Characters:
Ms. Jensen (company president, pushy, bossy)
Inventor (thinks he has finally created something worthwhile)
Droid (talks and walks mechanically)

Inventor is testing his invention, the world's first Christian droid.

INVENTOR: *(Looks over the droid)* Everything is set. Now for the one final test before Ms. Jensen arrives. *(Turns on switch.)*

DROID: Hello. My name is Naomi. May I help you?

INVENTOR: Please tell me what Romans 5:1 says.

DROID: Romans 5:1. Therefore, having been justified by faith, we have peace with God through our Lord Jesus Christ. Romans 5:1.

INVENTOR: Great. *(Pleased with himself)* I've done it. I'm a genius. Wait until Ms. Jensen sees this. She'll take back her threats of firing me. The ol' bat doesn't realize we geniuses need time to...

MS. JENSEN: *(Has entered room)* Mm-hmmmm.

INVENTOR: Oh, Ms. Jensen. Hi. I'm glad you could come to see this invention. I was just saying that a bat just flew—

MS. JENSEN: Never mind. Just get on with the demonstration.

INVENTOR: OK. Well, what you are looking at will revolutionize churches and the Christian community. It is a Christian droid, the perfect Christian for any situation. Its memory includes a complete concordance, a topical scripture index, and Greek and Hebrew recall. It can share the four spiritual laws, preach a sermon, and provide answers to Bible study questions. It will not swear, lie, or cheat.

MS. JENSEN: It sounds pretty impressive. May I try it?

INVENTOR: Of course.

DROID: Hello. My name is Naomi. May I help you?

MS. JENSEN: What passage of scripture says to "rejoice always?"

DROID: First Thessalonians 5:16.

MS. JENSEN: Give me a reference for a verse that will help me deal with stress.

DROID: Philippians 4:6.

MS. JENSEN: Excellent. *(To inventor)* Well, it seems like you've actually done something right. A Christian droid. It'd be a wonderful team member for Bible Trivia. Good work, Johnson. *(Exits.)*

INVENTOR: We did it! You, Naomi, are the perfect Christian.

DROID: *(The droid begins to break down. She starts talking faster with each successive line.)* Does not compute. I am a droid. I am designed to give appropriate Christian responses. I am not a Christian. I am a droid. I am not a Christian.

INVENTOR: But you are. You say and do—

DROID: Insufficient data. Romans 6:29. God designs *people* to be conformed to His image. I am not a man. I am a droid. Your design and purpose do not equal God's. Does not compute. Insufficient data. Does not compute. Overload. Overload. Overload. Overload. *(Droid moves about wildly for a moment, then collapses.)*

INVENTOR: No. No! I can't believe it. All my work is in these blown circuits. Now I've got to start all over. *(Resolves to begin again.)* Being a genius isn't easy.

LIGHTS

37
Spiritual Disguises

Topic:
God's Plan

Theme:
One key to successful Christian living is to spend time with God. We must put aside our spiritual disguises and allow God to use us as we are.

Scripture:
2 Corinthians 3:12-18
1 Timothy 4:12

Characters:
Salesperson
Sunbeam Model
"Better Than Bumper Stickers" Model
Kneeling Person
Unknown Christian

Props:
paper bag
bumper stickers
knee pads

SALESPERSON: Are you slowing down and fading fast in your Christian life? Have you got the ho-hums or the doldrums? Feeling a little less than holy? Well, I've got just what you need. I'm from Evangelical Veil Productions and we've got some great products for you. I've brought with me some of our newest designs. The first is our "Jesus Wants Me To Be A Sunbeam Model."

SUNBEAM MODEL: *(Smiling continuously)* Hi. No matter where I go or what I do, people know I'm a Christian because I'm so happy, always smiling. *(Shows off smile.)* See. Everyone will know you're one, too. Just $19.95 on sale today.

SALESPERSON: Thank you. Isn't that great? Our next model is the "Better Than Bumper Stickers Model."

"BETTER THAN BUMPER STICKERS" MODEL: Bumper stickers not enough to share your faith? Then try body stickers. Wear them all over. *(Putting stickers on)* On your arms, on your legs, everywhere. They are great. Just $12.95 for a package of six.

SALESPERSON: If that's not your style, we've got more. Perhaps you're looking for something more sophisticated. If so, you might want to try our kneeling pads. They enable you to kneel wherever you are: at play, at work, and at home.

KNEELING PERSON: I've been wearing these for two weeks now and they're the greatest—people think I'm praying wherever I go at play, at work, and at home. *(Walks off on knees, hands in prayerful position.)*

SALESPERSON: Just $18.95 for those. And, finally, for those of you who want to share your faith but are afraid of being recognized, we have the unknown Christian mask. *(Puts bag over head.)* Beneath this bag you can share your faith in perfect safety. *(Another person with bag over head walks in.)*

UNKNOWN CHRISTIAN: These don't work. Nobody cares what I say or do because they don't know who I am. And they don't make me feel any better, either. *(Takes off bag.)* If you really want to get rid of the ho-hums and doldrums, don't get an outer covering from Evangelical Veil Productions. Do spend time with God. Let his Spirit dwell in you. It'll make all the difference.

LIGHTS

38
What Can I Give Him?

Topic:
God's Plan

Theme:
Sometimes people try to buy their way into God's favor. However, what God wants cannot be bought or sold, only given.

Scripture:
Micah 6:6-8
Psalms 51:16,17
Mark 12:30
Romans 12:1

Characters:
Person

PERSON: *(Enters nervously carrying a few helium balloons.)* I hope He likes these. It's so hard to know what to get Him. I thought getting something for my mom last week was hard, but this is impossible. I mean what can you buy God?. It's not like He needs clothes or anything. What do you buy someone who owns the whole world? *(Looks up.)* Oh, hi. Happy Lord's day!

(Holding out balloons) These are for you. *(Lets go of balloons; they go flying. Disappointedly)* I guess they are not exactly what you wanted. *(Trying to think of something.)* Well...*(looking in pockets).* Here. My charge cards. Take them. Pick out something you'd like, anything. They take MasterCard everywhere. *(Realizing how ridiculous the idea is)* I guess you wouldn't want to do any shopping here, would you? *(Puts cards away and in doing so finds a lucky rabbit's foot.)* I know, my lucky rabbit's foot. Would you like my lucky rabbit's foot? *(No response. Despondently)* No. Well... *(Enthusiastic)* ...maybe you'd like something bigger. We have a small piece of property at Lake Tahoe. It's not developed or anything, but— *(Thinking better of idea)* I guess you don't really need a getaway place, do you? *(Depressed)* I don't know what I can give you, then. Everything I have I got from you. *(Listening)* My jacket? You want my jacket? *(Listening)* Oh, open my jacket. *(Pointing to heart)* You want what?. Well, I don't know. I mean you don't just give your heart to anybody. Then again, you're not just anybody. *(Thinks a second, then responds enthusiastically)* I'll do it. After all, if anybody can take care of it, you can.

LIGHTS

39
Ironclad Contract

Topic:
God's Promise

Theme:
When we commit ourselves to Jesus Christ by accepting Him as Lord and Savior, we are his heirs. His promises to us are great and eternal.

Scripture:
James 2:5
Galatians 5:22,23
John 10:10

Characters:
Becky
Jami

Props:
book
contract

Two friends meet at a park. Jami enters excitedly; Becky is reading a book.

JAMI: Becky, guess what? You won't believe what happened. I can hardly believe it myself. I just signed a contract with *the* top talent agency in the Bay Area. I am so excited.

BECKY: *(Genuinely happy for her)* That's great, Jami.

JAMI: The contract I signed is incredible. It's for ten years, for a minimum of two million dollars. Two million! Can you believe it? That's at least $200,000 a year! I'll be rich! I'll be famous! Me! Jami Whicker. Only that won't be my name anymore. I have a brand-new name. It's in my contract and everything. Chelsea Summer. *(As if doing her friend a favor)* But you can call me Chels.

BECKY: Thanks, Jami.

JAMI: *(Showing Becky contract)* Here it is, right here in black and white. And it's ironclad. For the next ten years they're stuck with me.

BECKY: *(Looking at the contract)* It sure looks good.

JAMI: Yep, I'm on my way! One day I'm nothing; the next I've got a new job, a new name, a new income. You just never know, do you? Hey, I've been so busy talking about myself I forgot to ask about you. How are you?

BECKY: Fine. *(Thinking)* You know, I have an ironclad contract, too!

JAMI: You do? You mean with your job at McDonalds?

BECKY: No, not with McDonalds. It's a lot better deal than that.

JAMI: *(Interested)* Really?

BECKY: It's a lifetime contract, and I know the other party won't back out on me.

JAMI: What do you get?

BECKY: All kinds of things are available to me, like I've got connections in every country in the world, and, although I'm not guaranteed an income, I am guaranteed things money can't buy, like: love, integrity, joy, and... *(trying to remember everything)* like you, I got a new name!

JAMI: *(Believing her friend is getting married)* Congratulations! You're getting married! That's wonderful! When's the big day?

BECKY: *(A little embarrassed)* No, I'm not getting married. My contract is with God. *(Proudly)* It's ironclad. He commits to me his strength, riches, and the power of his name, and I give Him my heart.

JAMI: Sounds like you got a good deal.

BECKY: I think so.

JAMI: You know, I thought I'd gotten quite a deal, but yours is even better. I'm going to have to talk to my agent about this.

LIGHTS

40
I'm Not Moving

Topic:
God's Will

Theme:
God's general will for people can be found in the Bible

Scripture:
1 John
Romans 10

Characters:
Julie (immobilized by her fear of not doing God's will)
Sara (helpful)

Julie is sitting stiffly in a chair. She appears afraid to move. Sara enters. Julie keeps looking straight ahead.

SARA: What are you doing?

JULIE: I'm sitting.

SARA: Have you been here long?

JULIE: *(Glancing at her watch)* Oh, about three hours.

SARA: Are you waiting for someone?

JULIE: No.

SARA: Then what are you doing?

JULIE: Nothing.

SARA: I can see that, but why?

JULIE: I'm afraid to do anything.

SARA: What are you afraid of?

JULIE: God. You see, I want to do God's will, but I'm afraid I won't. I don't know whether He wants me to stand up, or go for a walk, or go to the library, or do my grocery shopping, or pay my bills, or make an appointment with the dentist. I'm afraid that I'll do something He doesn't want me to do and then "poof," I'll be zapped.

SARA: I can tell you what God's will is.

JULIE: *(Stands up)* Really? How do you know?

SARA: God's will for everybody is pretty clear in the Bible.

JULIE: Well, what is it?

SARA: First, He wants everybody to know Him and to believe in his son, Jesus Christ, as Lord and Savior.

JULIE: Well, I do believe. I mean, I think I do, but I thought if I did I'd know what his will is, but I don't. I mean, how can you really know if you know Him? Wouldn't He tell me what to do if He really loved me?

SARA: But I told you, He has. There are general guidelines that govern his will for you, and if you follow them you'll know you know Him, and you'll know you're in his will.

JULIE: What are the guidelines?

SARA: Obeying his commandments, loving people the way He does, believing in Jesus, not sinning—

JULIE: *(Sits back down; looks straight ahead)* Now I know I'm never going to move.

SARA: Why?

JULIE: I can't possibly do all that.

SARA: Not by yourself, but if you let Him help you, you can. *(Grabs her by the arm)* Come on, I'm sure God's got something special planned for you today. *(They exit.)*

LIGHTS

41
The Will Scale

Topic:
God's Will

Theme:
We can get more direction about God's specific will if we follow these general principles: read the Scriptures, follow its directions, and pray.

Scripture:
1 Thessalonians 5:16-18
Psalms 1:2,3
James 1:22

Characters:
Person (represents all Christians seeking to know God)
Adversary (tries to get person to focus on selfish desires)
Advocate (tries to get person to realize that by being in God's will, it is easier to do God's will)

Props:
cardboard numbers 1 through 10

The cardboard numbers represent a scale that registers how close people are to being in God's will. Adversary, preferably dressed in dark colors, stands at #1. Advocate, dressed in light colors, stands at #10.

PERSON: This is a "will" scale. You're probably not familiar with this particular model, but I'm sure you'll be able to identify with how it works. When I'm at 10 on the scale, I'm doing God's will for me. When I'm at 1 on the scale, I'm ignoring God's will. Let me demonstrate. *(Person steps to #5.)* I've been offered a new job with a different company. I haven't been able to discern whether it's God's will for me to take it or not. My decision process has gone something like this.

ADVERSARY: Take it. It's a great chance to make a lot of money for a little effort.

PERSON: *(Moving to #3)* That's true.

ADVERSARY: You can have almost anything if you make enough money.

PERSON: *(Moving to #1)* You're right. I'll make the change.

ADVOCATE: What about the relationships you've developed at your present job? Don't they count for anything?

PERSON: I forgot about the people. And Mary has been asking so many questions about my relationship with God. *(Moving to #7)* Maybe I should stay where I am.

ADVERSARY: But there's so much room for advancement at the new job. With a little manipulation you could be vice-president in no time.

PERSON: *(Moving to #5)* Imagine me, a vice president. *(Daydreaming)* Vice president, I like that. *(Moves to #3.)*

ADVOCATE: But what about the commitment you made to your present company?

PERSON: *(Moving to #5)* I did say I'd stay there two more years.

ADVERSARY: So you lied. It's just a little white lie.

PERSON: *(Looking at Adversary and then Advocate)* Oh, I don't know.

ADVERSARY: You'd have enough money for a Maserati.

PERSON: *(Moving to #1)* I've always wanted a Maserati. I can just see me zooming to work in it now. But I wonder... *(moving to #5)* ...I wonder if that's what God wants.

ADVERSARY: He'll let you know if He doesn't.

(Person moves to #3.)

ADVOCATE: Maybe He already has.

PERSON:*(Moving to #5)* What do you mean?

ADVOCATE: You could follow the instructions He's already given you.

PERSON: *(Moving to #7)* What instructions?

ADVERSARY: You're not going to say, "Read the Bible," are you?

ADVOCATE: Why not?

ADVERSARY: Nobody should read that anymore. It's totally outdated. Besides, it doesn't say anything about Maseratis.

ADVOCATE: But it does say something about God's will.

PERSON: What?

ADVOCATE: That you should be saved, spirit-filled, sanctified, willing to suffer, submissive, and thankful.

PERSON: All that? Can a person really be all that?

ADVOCATE: Yes, and if you decide to become God's will, you'll find that doing God's will is much easier.

PERSON: Anything's got to be easier than going back and forth like this. I'm going to try it.

LIGHTS

42
The Flight

Topic:
Holy Spirit

Theme:
The Holy Spirit is God and lives inside Christians.

Scripture:
Acts 5:3-5
John 14:15-18,23-24

Characters:
First Passenger
Second Passenger

Two passengers are on an airplane, talking.

FIRST PASSENGER: Do you ever think that the only thing holding up this airplane is air?

SECOND PASSENGER: I try not to.

FIRST PASSENGER: Well, do you ever wonder what the chances are that this plane might be hijacked?

SECOND PASSENGER: I try not to, especially when I'm in it.

FIRST PASSENGER: Well, do you ever wonder about the pilot?

SECOND PASSENGER: What do you mean?

FIRST PASSENGER: Do you ever wonder whether he's had a few drinks before he comes to work?

SECOND PASSENGER: Not until now. Are you afraid of flying?

FIRST PASSENGER: *(Not willing to admit it)* Me? No. *(Hoping Second Passenger is)* Are you?

SECOND PASSENGER: Not really.

FIRST PASSENGER: I bet if you thought of all the things that could go wrong, you'd be afraid.

SECOND PASSENGER: I don't think so. I've got a Counselor I can talk to.

FIRST PASSENGER: Oh, well I couldn't afford to see a counselor about my fears.

SECOND PASSENGER: This counselor doesn't charge for the services. In fact, the Counselor lives with me.

FIRST PASSENGER: Must be a very special person. Is it your spouse?

SECOND PASSENGER: I think I've given you the wrong impression. My Counselor is the Holy Spirit.

FIRST PASSENGER: The Holy what?

SECOND PASSENGER: The Holy Spirit.

FIRST PASSENGER: You're not one of the *Out On A Branch* people, are you? *(Scooting away from Second Passenger)* A 250,000-year-old man doesn't speak from you, does he?

SECOND PASSENGER: No. The Holy Spirit is God.

FIRST PASSENGER: *(Skeptical)* And this "Holy Spirit" lives inside you?

SECOND PASSENGER: That's right.

FIRST PASSENGER: Are you on any illegal substance?

SECOND PASSENGER: No.

FIRST PASSENGER: And you're serious?

SECOND PASSENGER: Absolutely.

FIRST PASSENGER: I'd like to hear more.

SECOND PASSENGER: Well, we've got a long flight ahead.

FIRST PASSENGER: I hope so.

LIGHTS

43
The Helper

Topic:
Holy Spirit

Theme:
To be the people whom God intends us to be, we must be continually filled with the Holy Spirit.

Scripture:
Ephesians 5:18
Romans 8:5,6
Galatians 5:18-25

Characters:
Three nine-year-old girls: Janie, Suzy, and Mary

Props:
jacks

The three girls are playing jacks.

JANIE: Have you ever heard of the Holy Spirit?

SUZY: The what?

JANIE: The Holy Spirit.

SUZY: No, what is it?

MARY: My mom says you should always be filled with the Holy Spirit.

SUZY: *(Not understanding)* How much do you have to eat before you get full?

JANIE: *(Laughing at Suzy's ignorance)* You don't eat it, silly. He's a person, and my dad says He's our helper.

MARY: I haven't seen any Holy Spirit helping me clean my room lately. What kind of helper is he if he won't do that?

JANIE: I think He's supposed to help us be more like God.

MARY: Does he help with homework?

JANIE: I don't think so.

SUZY: Well, how much do you have to pay him for his help?

JANIE: *(Know it all)* You don't pay Him, you just ask Him and then He helps you.

MARY: Really?

JANIE: Yep.

SUZY: *(Starting to get the idea)* Can the Holy Spirit help me not hit my brother?

JANIE: I think so, but you've got to want to not hit him, too.

SUZY: *(Disappointed)* Oh.

MARY: Well, what about sharing? Can the Holy Spirit help me share my toys? I get in so much trouble for being selfish.

JANIE: I think He can.

SUZY: Are you sure the Holy Spirit can make people more like God?

JANIE: Yeah.

SUZY: Then how come the world isn't a nicer place, huh? How come more people don't act nice, like God?

JANIE: Maybe they forget to ask the Holy Spirit for help.

SUZY: *(Determined)* Well, when I grow up, I'm going to remember to ask the Holy Spirit to help me be more like God.

JANIE: *(Enthusiastically)* Me too! I'm gonna ask a hundred times a day 'cause I really want to be like Him.

MARY: Well, I'm gonna ask a *zillion* times a day.

SUZY: Then I'm going to ask a million zillion times a day.

JANIE: I don't think we're acting much like God now.

SUZY: I guess it's going to take a while for us to get the hang of this.

JANIE: Yeah, so it's a good thing we're starting now.

(All exit.)

LIGHTS

44
Surrender

Topic:
Holy Spirit

Theme:
As Christians we allow the Holy Spirit to save us. But too often we don't allow the Spirit to show us what God intends for us to do. We need to learn to surrender to the Spirit so He can teach, equip, and empower us.

Scripture:
John 16:12,13
John 14:25,26
1 Peter 4:10
Ephesians 5:17,18

Characters:
Sam
Jane

Props:
white flag

A mock battlefield. Sam and Jane are in a foxhole.

JANE: I hate all this fighting. Why doesn't God make it easier for us to be on his side?

SAM: Because we're people with minds of our own.

JANE: But we're not smarter than He is, are we?

SAM: Of course not.

JANE: That's what I thought. Then I'm going to do it. *(Puts flag together.)*

SAM: What are you going to do?

JANE: I'm going to surrender.

SAM: Why? It's not even over yet.

JANE: It is for me. I'm tired of acting like I know more, that *his* way is too simple, that his way will get me nowhere. The truth is *my* way is getting me nowhere. I'm surrendering to the Spirit's teaching.

SAM: But then you'll have to do things his way. Think of your job. You'll have to be honest—no more little white lies.

JANE: No more big black ones either.

SAM: You'll lose money.

JANE: There's more to life than money. We both know that.

SAM: *(Putting hand on Jane's forehead)* I think you must be suffering from battle fatigue. Medic! Medic!

JANE: I just want to surrender. Then I can have his fire power. Once I see life from his point of view, I might be a winner.

SAM: But if you surrender, that means you lose.

JANE: No, if I surrender, I win. *(Begins to exit with flag.)*

SAM: Who knows? Maybe she's right. I could use a break from all this fighting. *(Begins to follow Jane.)*

LIGHTS

45
I'm Not Going to Try It

Topic:
Husbands

Theme:
Husbands are supposed to love their wives as Christ loves the church. Husbands are to support them, sacrifice for them, cherish them, and serve them.

Scripture:
Ephesians 5:22-30

Characters:
Fred
John
Mike

Three men have just finished a Bible study.

FRED: *(Pushing Bible to John)* I'm not going to try it.

JOHN: *(Pushing Bible to Mike)* You try it.

MIKE: *(Pushing it to Fred)* Not me.

FRED: I'm not going to try it.

JOHN: Well, somebody's got to try it.

FRED: It's not going to be me.

MIKE: Then we'll never know if it'll make our marriages better or not.

FRED: Of course it would. Everything else He said works.

JOHN: I know, I know.

FRED: I'm not going to be the one to apply eighty chapters of scripture to my life.

MIKE: Is that how many chapters of the Bible have scripture about Jesus and the church?

JOHN: Yep. And there's no way I can love my wife the way Christ loves the church.

MIKE: Think of it as a challenge.

JOHN: *You* think of it as a challenge.

MIKE: *(Opening the Bible)* Look, all that we really have to do is support our wives, sacrifice for them, cherish them, and serve them. *(Not really believing what he's saying)* It's no problem.

JOHN and FRED: *(Sarcastically)* Right.

MIKE: OK, it's a problem. But we're still supposed to do it.

FRED: Why do we have to do God's will when our wives aren't?

MIKE: Well, how can we expect them to do it if we won't? I'm going to try it.

FRED: Good, you try it, Mike, and if it works out for you and Helen, I'll try it.

MIKE: *(Exiting)* Right.

JOHN: I like that Mikey. He'll try anything.

LIGHTS

46
Guess Who's Coming to Dinner

Topic:
Hypocrisy

Theme:
If Jesus came to our house for dinner, we might be embarrassed by our casual, half-hearted Christian lifestyle. We need to live each day knowing our heart is his home.

Scripture:
Galatians 2:20
John 14:23
Romans 8:9-14

Characters:
Jami (a homemaker)

Props:
phone
National Enquirer
potato chips

Jami is reading the National Enquirer and eating potato chips when she receives an unexpected phone call.

JAMI: *(Picking up telephone)* Hello? Oh, hi, honey. You got a new business partner? That's wonderful. *(Surprised)* He's God? That's even more wonderful. *(Not so excited)* You're bringing Him home for dinner? Tonight? But honey, tonight isn't a good night. The house is a mess and there isn't anything to eat in the refrigerator, but... You're sure you can't change His mind? OK. Bye. *(Not too enthusiastically)* I love you, too. *(Hangs up phone.)*

God is coming to my house for dinner and look at this place. It's a disaster area. I'll never be able to clean this up in an hour. I should have told John, "No! There is absolutely no way God can come tonight." But then John would have had to tell God that, and God might not have liked that and... *(Sighs)* Oh, well... *(Getting an idea)* I know! I'll put the car in the garage, turn out all the lights, and pretend I'm not home, and then maybe John will take Him out to dinner. Then again, maybe John will use his key and come in and find me in all this mess. *(Resigns herself)* I guess there's no way around it. God is coming here for dinner.

Now, let's see. I've got to vacuum, and dust, do the dishes... *(All of a sudden remembering)* Oh, in the kitchen, there's that Beautiful Buns calendar. I don't know if God would approve of that. And there are a couple of magazines under the bed I'd better get rid of. Oh, and those books in the family room. They aren't exactly X-rated, but I'll hide them just in case. And our tax return is on the desk; I don't want Him to suspect we're cheating on our taxes. I'd better just keep God downstairs. Upstairs is too difficult to clean. *(Sits down.)*

Boy, I'm going to have to be awfully careful about how I treat John. I don't want God to think I'm a bad wife. I'll just have to be extra nice and watch my mouth.

Oh, that's the phone again. *(Picks up the phone)* Hello? What? God's going to stay here overnight? Indefinitely overnight? But, wouldn't God be happier staying somewhere else? You're sure that's what God wants? OK. *(Desperately)* But stall him as long as you can. Bye! *(Hangs up phone.)*

(Gets an idea) I know. I'll put everything I don't want God to see in the upstairs closet and lock it. Then tomorrow when God leaves for work with John, I'll burn it in the fireplace. That's what I'll do. Well, it's been nice talking to you, but as you can see, I've got lots to do!

LIGHTS

47
Middle Ground

Topic:
Identity in Christ

Theme:
We must choose to be either in the world or in Christ. It is impossible to be in both.

Scripture:
Ephesians 1:4-12
Romans 8:29

Characters:
World
Kingdom
Person

Props: (Optional)
world, in worldly attire
kingdom
angel hat

WORLD: Leave her alone.

KINGDOM: No! She has to make up her mind. She's either a citizen *in* Christ or *in* the world.

PERSON: But why can't I be in both? You know, take the best from both worlds.

KINGDOM: Because a person whose identity is *in* Christ cannot be in the world.

PERSON: But I'd be an outcast if I did everything God's way.

KINGDOM: And you don't feel like one now?

PERSON: Of course I do. But I won't. I mean, I just need to make a few more friends and a lot more money. Then I'll fit right in.

WORLD: Give the woman a chance. She'll be fitting in very well before too long.

KINGDOM: Really? Like at that party last week?

PERSON: What party? *(Realizing the party being talked about)* You know about the party?

KINGDOM: *He* knows everything.

WORLD: She didn't do anything wrong at the party.

KINGDOM: She lied.

WORLD: *So what?* Everybody lies.

PERSON: *(Rationalizing)* Besides, I only lied so I wouldn't have to use cocaine. I knew God would disapprove of that.

KINGDOM: But you didn't tell anybody at the party anything about God.

WORLD: Of course she didn't. If she had, she probably would have been laughed right out of the room.

PERSON: *(Protesting the inference that she did something wrong)* I held on to my values.

KINGDOM: You compromised your values by lying.

WORLD: So she told them she'd done a few lines and didn't want to overindulge. What's the harm in letting them think she uses cocaine?

KINGDOM: She acted like she wanted to be in the world. If she wants to do that, she's not in Christ.

PERSON: But I don't want to be in the world. You don't know how it is. I mean, everywhere I go people are talking about things that oppose Christ's way.

KINGDOM: Like in the park yesterday?

PERSON: You know about the park?

WORLD: They are everywhere.

KINGDOM: It was the perfect opportunity to share your faith.

WORLD: You didn't really expect her to talk to that woman who was channeling.

PERSON: I was so tired. I've been working lots of overtime to try to save enough money for a new BMW.

WORLD: She's just trying to keep up with the Joneses.

PERSON: I'm just trying to survive.

KINGDOM: Is that all you want to do: survive?

PERSON: Isn't that all there is?

WORLD: Yes, that's all there is.

KINGDOM: Not if she chooses to have her citizenship in the kingdom. Then there's security, forgiveness, purpose, destiny, a sense of belonging...

PERSON: *(To Kingdom)* I think I'd better go with you.

LIGHTS

48
The Audience

Topic:
Jesus' Deity

Theme:
Jesus is God. He didn't come just as a representative, or as a substitute for God, but was, and is, God.

Scripture:
John 5:14-18; 8:15-69
Matthew 14:59-61; 26:62-66

Characters:
Joanne and Phil Jones (two social snobs)
Tami (a friend of the Joneses)

Props:
book

TAMI: *(Looking up from her book)* Uh-oh, here come the Joneses. It's absolutely impossible to keep up with them. They seem to have it all. *(Hides behind book.)* Maybe they won't notice me.

JOANNE: Tami! Tami! Is that you? I'm so glad we ran into you. I wanted to let you know about our latest adventure.

TAMI: You've already told me about your trip around the world.

JOANNE: But we've added one more stop.

PHIL: Right after our stay in the Alps we're going straight into the heavens.

JOANNE: We're going to have a *private* audience with God.

PHIL: We've prepared for any obstacle we might run into. We've taken scuba lessons in case He's surrounded by water. We've taken courses in self-defense in case there are armed guards. We learned hang gliding in case we need to fly in, and we brought an extra million dollars just in case we need to bribe someone.

TAMI: But you don't have to go to all that trouble to talk to God.

JOANNE: We even learned mountain climbing.

PHIL: We figure if Moses had to, we might, too.

TAMI: But you can have a private audience with God and never leave home.

JOANNE: Really?

PHIL: *(To Joanne)* She probably means with Jesus, and we're not interested in any middleman. We want to go to the head honcho!

TAMI: But they are the same; Jesus is God.

PHIL: You mean Jesus is *like* God.

TAMI: No, I mean Jesus is God.

PHIL: You mean Jesus is God's son.

TAMI: No, I mean Jesus is God.

PHIL: Are you sure?

TAMI: The Bible makes it quite clear. Jesus is God.

PHIL: You mean we can speak with Him here and now.

TAMI: And anytime you like.

PHIL: That's amazing. I wish I'd known. We could have saved a lot of money.

JOANNE: *(A little upset)* That means I learned how to repel down cliffs for nothing!

PHIL: How was I supposed to know that Jesus and God are the same?

JOANNE: You could read your Bible once in a while.

PHIL: So could you.

LIGHTS

49
Getting Off the Fence

Topic:
Lifestyle

Theme:
Being a Christian means having security, forgiveness, God's unconditional love, a purpose for living, and a destiny. If we are hypocritical in our lifestyle, we will not be able to experience God's gifts to us.

Scripture:
Ephesians 1:4-12
1 John 2:15-17

Characters:
Person

PERSON: I know what it's like trying to be a Christian in the world. I've tried it and it isn't easy. In fact, being a Christian and *in* the world is impossible. I'll show you what I mean.

(When the person is talking to the right, he or she is talking to God. When the person is talking to the left, he or she is talking to someone in the world.)

(To the left) Now, you're sure the IRS won't question this deduction? I mean, I didn't really contribute that much, and I don't have a receipt. Are you sure everybody does it? OK, if you're sure.

(To the right) You heard him, Lord. Everybody else does it. I mean, why should I pay more taxes than everybody else?

(To the left) You really can get me in for free? And you're sure your boss doesn't mind? What do you mean, he'll never know?

(To the right) I know I shouldn't have snuck in the back door, but the tickets were so expensive, and I really wanted to see the show. Who knows? It might be a good conversation starter. It might even lead to sharing my faith.

(To the left) No, I wasn't reading a Bible. Why would I be reading a Bible? This book is a dictionary. I'm trying to improve my vocabulary.

(To the right) I'm sorry, Lord. I didn't tell them because they just don't understand. Remember last week when they asked me to go bar hopping and I couldn't because I had Bible study, but I lied and told them I had a date? It's just like that.

(To audience) So I lived like that for quite a while, saying one thing to God and doing another. Then one day somebody called me a hypocrite. I was really angry until I realized it was true. I was a hypocrite.

Did I really want to be a Christian? Why did I become one in the first place? God offered me things I couldn't get in the world. He loved me, He forgave me, and He even gave me a purpose for living.

I lost sight of that while I was sitting on the fence. So I decided to get off the fence. That seemed simple enough until I did it. Since I wasn't going to be hypocritical any more, I had to be honest. It was even more uncomfortable than sitting on the fence—but the benefits are much better.

LIGHTS

50
Lover's Day

Topic:
Love

Theme:
To love Jesus we must love as he does: unselfishly, sincerely, and sacrificially.

Scripture:
John 21

Characters:
Hubby
Wife

Props:
newspaper
magazine

Hubby is reading newspaper. Wife enters with current issue of Lover's Day.

WIFE: There's the greatest little test in my current issue of *Lover's Day*. I want you to take it. *(Sits down, pencil in hand.)* Question One: You are fifteen minutes late for an appointment. On your way to the appointment, you see someone you know, but you don't really like, who is having trouble changing a flat tire. Do you: a) wave as you go by; b) pretend you don't see them; or c) stop and help them fix the flat?

HUBBY: I don't think I want to take this test.

WIFE: I'll go to Question Two. It's easier. Your son comes home from school with an "A" on his algebra test. He tells you that he copied all his answers from his girlfriend's paper. You: a) congratulate him and give him the car keys; b) tell him never to do it again; or c) ground him and make him turn himself in.

HUBBY: *(Proud of himself)* I can get that one. "C."

WIFE: Question Three: You turn on TV and there is a special about world hunger. They say that every two seconds a child dies of hunger. You: a) change the channel; b) decide you'll pray for the hungry in the world; or c) ask God how you can help and become involved in solving the problem of world hunger.

HUBBY: You know, I don't think I want to take this test. It's making me feel uncomfortable.

WIFE: Just a couple more. Four: You have just finished a shopping spree with your eight-year-old. On your way to your BMW you see a transient panhandling. You: a) shield your child from them and ignore them completely; b) drop your spare change in their cup; or c) buy him a sandwich.

HUBBY: *(Changing the subject)* Is there anything good on TV?

WIFE: Come on, just one more. This is a great one. You wake up because the baby is crying at 3 a.m. Your wife is sleeping soundly. Do you a) wake your spouse by "accidentally" kicking her and then roll over and pretend you're asleep; b) get up to take care of the baby but make a lot of noise, enough to ensure that your spouse knows your are sacrificing your sleep for her; or c) quietly get up and take care of the baby?

HUBBY: What is this test supposed to show?

WIFE: How great a lover you are. Jesus loved unselfishly, sincerely, and sacrificially. We're supposed to love like that, too.

HUBBY: Oh. Well, don't bother adding up my scores. I think I know how well I didn't do.

LIGHTS

51
The Dinner

Topic:
Love

Theme:
God is the source of real love. To keep love alive in our hearts and life, He must be Lord.

Scripture:
1 John 4:9-12
John 3:16
Romans 5:5

Characters:
Hubby
Wife

Props:
two candles
small table

A romantic dinner by candlelight

HUBBY: This dinner is not turning out like I planned.

WIFE: I know. I thought we were going to have this wonderfully romantic dinner.

HUBBY: There'd be great food, great conversation, no children, no interruptions, and no arguments.

WIFE: Well, we've got everything but the conversation.

HUBBY: I never thought we'd run out of things to say to each other.

WIFE: Me neither. Remember when we were first married? We'd stay up til midnight talking.

HUBBY: Our lives were different then.

WIFE: You used to bring me daisies every Thursday.

HUBBY: And you'd send me cards at the office.

WIFE: And once a month we'd get up early and watch the sunrise.

HUBBY: I remember.

WIFE: We never ran out of things to say to each other then.

HUBBY: We had big dreams. We were going to make the world a better place.

WIFE: We were going to share Christ with all our neighbors and friends.

HUBBY: Remember that first neighborhood Bible study?

WIFE: How could I forget? It was just you and me for the first three weeks. What's happened to us?

HUBBY: I guess we got caught up in the rat race.

WIFE: And ended up a couple of rats.

HUBBY: You know, I miss the cards.

WIFE: I miss the daisies.

HUBBY: We've really botched things up. Maybe we should let the Lord be in charge like we used to.

WIFE: I was a lot happier then.

HUBBY: Me, too.

WIFE: We could get back to our original dream.

HUBBY: We could even start a neighborhood Bible study again.

WIFE: It'd be great. We could invite...

LIGHTS

52
The Locked Bathroom

Topic:
Marriage

Theme:
To communicate effectively we must: 1) lovingly confront rather than retreat; 2) try to listen; and 3) be quick to forgive.

Scripture:
1 Peter 4:8
Ephesians 4:31,32

Characters:
Jen
Carol

Props: (optional)
sign for marriage enrichment seminar

CAROL: Hi, Jen. What are you doing out here all alone?

JEN: Trying to decide whether or not I should go in.

CAROL: What happened?

JEN: Mark and I had a big fight. I don't know whether I can make myself go into the Marriage Enrichment Seminar alone. Everyone would know that we didn't learn anything last week. I feel like such a failure.

CAROL: I'm sorry.

JEN: It was all Mark's fault. Yesterday was our anniversary so I made a really special dinner. I cooked all of his favorites. I got fresh flowers and set the table with china and candles. I got dressed in this absolutely incredible red dress. When he came to the door, I greeted him with a kiss. He looked at me strangely, sat down on the couch, opened his briefcase, took out the paper, and asked me when dinner would be ready.

CAROL: So what did you do?

JEN: Well, I wasn't going to be the one to tell him he forgot our anniversary, so I turned off the roast, blew out the candles, and locked myself in the bathroom.

CAROL: What did he do?

JEN: Well, after what seemed like an eternity, he asked me what was wrong. So I told him, "Nothing," which, of course, he knows means "Everything." He was persistent, so I finally told him that it was our anniversary. Of course he immediately started apologizing and telling me how he'd been under a lot of pressure at work, so wouldn't I please come out of the bathroom? So I turned on the shower.

CAROL: You're kidding.

JEN: No, I didn't want to hear any apology because then I'd have to forgive him. I wanted him to suffer, so I spent the night in the bathroom.

CAROL: You know, if you were getting a grade on how you've applied the things we've learned at the seminar, you'd get an "F."

JEN: *(Defensively)* It was Mark's fault.

CAROL: But you didn't lovingly confront him with what he did. You retreated.

JEN: I did not.

CAROL: You locked yourself in the bathroom.

JEN: All right. I retreated.

CAROL: And you didn't even try to listen. You turned on the shower.

JEN: But—

CAROL: But we're supposed to listen to one another. *And*, you didn't even consider forgiving him. We're supposed to be quick to forgive.

JEN: I know, but it's a lot easier to say we should confront, listen, and forgive than it is to do it.

CAROL: I think you're going to have another chance. Here comes Mark. See you inside.

LIGHTS

53
The Separation

Topic:
Marriage

Theme:
Men and women have specific needs that need to be recognized and honored in marital relationships.

Scripture:
1 Peter 3:1-9
Ephesians 5:24-30

Characters:
Hubby
Wife

---

*Hubby and Wife are on stage opposite each other.
They are talking to audience, unaware of each other.*

HUBBY: I don't know why it happened. It was an ordinary morning. I was drinking my coffee and reading my paper. All of a sudden she says, "Steve, I want a trial separation." I thought she was kidding so I kept reading the paper. But when I asked for more coffee she was gone. She walked right out the door, just like that; she didn't even tell me what I did wrong.

WIFE: I told him hundreds of times what was wrong. He just wasn't listening. That's why I had to leave. He never listened. I was someone who cooked, cleaned, did laundry, and that's about all. When he told me he loved me, it wasn't convincing. It was the only thing he could think of to say.

HUBBY: It's not like I never told her I loved her. I was always telling her I loved her. She's crazy to walk out on me. But if she's going to act like that, maybe I'll be better off. It's not like I really *need* her. I can always get a maid. I never liked her lasagna anyway. She put too much garlic in it, and she wasn't that good at ironing. I just can't figure out why she left. What'd she want from me, anyway?

WIFE: You know what I really wanted? I wanted him to ask me how my day went and mean it. I wanted him to take time just for me to talk about what I was thinking and feeling. And I wanted him to remember why he married me. I wanted him to show me he still loved me, bring me a flower, take me on a picnic, or send me a card—anything out of the ordinary that would have let me know that, if he had to do it all over again, he'd still marry me.

HUBBY: She's the best thing that ever happened to me, and I let her walk right out the door. I'm miserable. The house is so empty. I guess you never really know what you have until you lose it. But maybe it's not too late. Maybe I can learn to love her, maybe I can even learn to listen.

WIFE: I'm going home. I think he's learning to listen. And I think I'm learning I'm not always right. Maybe we can learn to really love each other, with God's help.

LIGHTS

54
The Tennis Game

Topic:
Marriage

Theme:
In order for the marriage relationship to function the way
God intended it, both partners must follow God's instructions. If marriage was a tennis game, the players would
play to each other's strengths rather than against one
another or alone.

Scripture:
Proverbs 12:4; 18:22; 31:10-31
Ephesians 5:23-25

Characters:
Hubby
Wife

Props:
two tennis racquets

*A tennis court. Hubby and Wife mime tennis move-
ments.*

HUBBY: What kind of a serve was that?

WIFE: A great one. *You* have just been aced.

HUBBY: Are you blind? That ball wasn't even in the court.

WIFE: It was right on the line. I saw it plain as day.

HUBBY: You're crazy. It was out by a foot. Serve it again.

WIFE: It was in!

HUBBY: *(Even more adamantly)* Serve it again or we're going home.

WIFE: All right, you big baby!

HUBBY: Just serve it. *(As she serves)* Finally. *(He hits it back.)*

WIFE: *What* was that?

HUBBY: A lob.

WIFE: That was not a lob. It was a flob. That's the kind of stroke beginners make all the time.

HUBBY: I might as well play with a beginner. They're just as good as you are.

WIFE: At least you'd be at the same level.

HUBBY: Very funny.

WIFE: I'm serious.

HUBBY: Get the ball. It's my serve.

WIFE: No, it's not. That, and I quote, "lob" was not in the court.

HUBBY: *(Fed up)* You're an idiot.

WIFE: Then you're a super-idiot!

HUBBY: Sticks and stones may break my bones, but words will never hurt me.

WIFE: Well, this tennis racket might, honey.

HUBBY: I'm going home.

WIFE: Fine! I'll probably have more fun playing by myself anyway.

(Lights flash out for a moment. When they come back on, Wife is sitting with head in hands and Hubby is approaching.)

WIFE: I thought you went home.

HUBBY: I almost did, but I realized I didn't really want to be home alone. I'm sorry. I don't know what got into me.

WIFE: I'm sorry, too. It's just a game.

HUBBY: But we play it off the courts, too. I think it's time to stop playing against one another and maybe get on the same team.

WIFE: We do know each other's strengths and weaknesses.

HUBBY: I think we'd be a lot better off playing as partners.

WIFE: Me, too!

LIGHTS

55

The Miracle

Topic:
Miracles

Theme:
Miracles, though not probable, are possible. However, the greatest miracle of all we can experience is being born again by developing a relationship with our Creator.

Scripture:
1 Peter 1:3-9

Characters:
Sue (a Christian eager to share her faith
Sam (afraid of flying, caught in materialistic rat race)

Sam is sitting nervously on an airplane. Sue enters and sits next to him.

SUE: Are you nervous about flying?

SAM: Y...y...yes. How could you tell?

SUE: Well, for one thing, your knees are knocking.

SAM: I hate flying. It's a miracle I'm even on this flight. I've got this business meeting in New York. I didn't have the time to take the train, which is usually what I do, so I ended up having to take the plane, which I never do, so that's why it's a miracle I'm here.

SUE: *(Keying in on the word "miracle")* Oh, do you believe in miracles?

SAM: I just told you, it's a miracle I'm even on this plane.

SUE: I mean real—

SAM: I can't stop thinking that this huge mass of metal is supported by nothing but air. Have you ever thought about that? Nothing but air.

SUE: A simple course in physics would help you realize that we're perfectly safe.

SAM: I don't think so. Like I said, it's a miracle I'm on this plane.

SUE: So then you *do* believe in miracles.

SAM: I just told you I did.

SUE: I mean *real* miracles: events that defy natural law, that reveal divine intervention.

SAM: I think that there is a rational explanation for any so-called "miracles." Natural laws are unbreakable.

SUE: *I* believe in miracles.

SAM: You're not involved with one of those television ˥aith healers, are you? I am not an actor, and I would ˌt be interested in any kind of show like that.

SUE: I'm not involved with anything like that.

SAM: So you think those healers are frauds, too?

SUE: I don't know. Like I said, I believe in miracles, and although they are not probable, they *are* possible. Some of those faith healers could be authentic, and some of them could be fakes, but there are other kinds of miracles.

SAM: Like what?

SUE: Well, God's worked a miracle in my life.

SAM: What'd He do? Make you rich? Heal you of some fatal disease?

SUE: No, but He has given me purpose and meaning for my life. He's taught me that I'm worth a lot to Him, not because of anything I've ever done, but just because I'm one of his creations.

SAM: *(Skeptically)* You're kidding.

SUE: No, I mean it.

SAM: Well, it'd be a miracle if He could do that for me.

SUE: Miracles *do* happen.

SAM: Why don't you tell me more?

SUE: OK. You see, I was working sixteen-hour...

LIGHTS

56
Rainy Day

Topic:
Pain and Suffering

Theme:
Pain and suffering can help us be sensitized to others, and they can help build our character. They are a reality we cannot deny and often cannot explain.

Scripture:
James 1:2-5
1 Peter 4:12,13

Characters:
Two ten-year-old girls, Janie and Toni

Two children are playing inside because of the rain.
They are staring out a window.

JANIE: I hate the rain.

TONI: Me, too!

JANIE: And I hate having to play inside all day.

TONI: Me, too!

JANIE: There's nothing to do.

TONI: Nothing.

JANIE: I wonder why it rains.

TONI: Me, too!

JANIE: I think it has to be with atmospheric conditions.

TONI: What?

JANIE: You know, water and air and clouds and stuff like that.

TONI: Oh. I think it rains because God cries. The rain is God's tears.

JANIE: Why would God cry?

TONI: Because of all the hurting in the world.

JANIE: Why doesn't He just stop the hurting?

TONI: I don't know.

JANIE: Maybe He can't.

TONI: Of course He can. God can do anything.

JANIE: Then why doesn't He stop it?

TONI: Because...because...Well, I don't know exactly, but there must be a reason for it.

JANIE: Like what?

TONI: Well, hurts help us care for each other.

JANIE: I guess so.

TONI: And they help us to be better people.

JANIE: Do you really think so?

TONI: *(Shrugs)* Well, my mom says they build my character.

JANIE: Well, I hate it.

TONI: Me, too.

JANIE: And I hate it when God cries.

TONI: Me, too!

LIGHTS

57
A Wrong Way

Topic:
Prayer

Theme:
Prayer is not just a way for people to get what they want from God. It is a way for people to get to know God and his will for them better.

Scripture:
Matthew 21:12-17

Characters:
Jesse
Terry
Jill
Chris

Props:
catalog

JESSE: *(Reading from catalog)* And then I'd like the golf clubs on page 98; the compact disc player on page 10;

the big screen on 105; and the video recorder on page 106. If you could get those delivered by Friday, I'd really appreciate it. Amen.

TERRY: *(Kneeling)* And that girl, Shari, at the office is really causing me a problem because she's always talking about me behind my back, so if you could get her fired, I'd really appreciate it. And this pain in my back seems to be getting worse, so if you could heal that. And then my car needs brakes, and you know I can't afford to get them fixed, so if you could...

JILL: Lord, I haven't had a date in three weeks, and you've had my specifications for three years. I really am tired of waiting. I want an affluent, good-looking man who loves children, and, of course, you. *And*, if he could call by...

CHRIS: *(Who has been watching all of this)* I can't believe how selfish you all are. All of your prayers are about yourselves and your own problems.

JESSE: And I suppose you don't ask God for things.

CHRIS: Of course I do, but only in emergencies. Like when I got in a car accident last week, and when I almost got bitten by a rattlesnake two years ago when I was backpacking, or when I swam out too far and started to get cramps.

TERRY: So you think of God as your personal bodyguard?

CHRIS: Well, sort of.

JILL: That seems pretty selfish to me.

CHRIS: *(To Jill)* At least I think of Him as more than a matchmaker.

JILL: *(To Terry)* Well, I think of Him as more than a mechanic.

TERRY: *(To Jesse)* Well, I think of Him as more than a catalog clerk.

JESSE: I never really thought of it as if I was treating Him like a catalog clerk. I bet He doesn't like it.

TERRY: He probably doesn't think much of being a mechanic, either.

JILL: Or a matchmaker.

CHRIS: Or a bodyguard.

JESSE: But I don't know how else to pray. Do you think He would send me instructions if I asked?

TERRY: He already has.

JILL: You mean the Bible?

TERRY: Right.

CHRIS: Maybe we could learn together. You want to try?

TERRY, JESSE, and JILL: Sure!

LIGHTS

58

Interpreters of the Lord's Prayer

Topic:
Prayer

Theme:
An understanding of the Lord's Prayer will help us know
it's value in our prayer life.

Scripture:
Matthew 6:7-13

Characters:
First Person
Second Person
Third Person

Props:
a long list

---

*Three people are in a horizontal line. (Note: This is a
Reader's Theatre-style presentation, but lines must be
memorized. However, during certain portions, characters must be real characters.)*

FIRST PERSON: And He said to them, "When you pray, say, 'Father hallowed be thy name, Thy kingdom come.' "

SECOND PERSON: He's not just secretary of the treasury.

THIRD PERSON: *(Pretends to be praying)* Since you own the cattle on a thousand hills, I was wondering if you wouldn't mind selling them. There are a few things I'd like to buy. *(Pulls out list.)* A sailboat, a beach house in Malibu, a...

FIRST PERSON: And He's not the chief investigator for the FBI.

SECOND PERSON: Where were you on the night of January 15, 1962? Have you ever cheated? What about that spelling test in Mrs. Burns' class?

THIRD PERSON: *(Protesting)* That was in the fourth grade.

SECOND PERSON: It all counts.

FIRST PERSON: He's our Father.

SECOND PERSON: Not an evil dictator or a spiteful judge.

THIRD PERSON: Our Father, with a father's heart and a father's love.

SECOND PERSON: If we remember that, we'll worship Him.

FIRST PERSON: "Give us each day our daily bread."

SECOND PERSON: We ask God to meet our physical needs.

THIRD PERSON: We take this for granted with our ritualistic grace.

FIRST PERSON: "Pass the bread and pass the meat. Pitch in, all you fools, and eat."

SECOND PERSON: Do you mean what you say?

THIRD PERSON: Are you asking for what you need?

FIRST PERSON: Do you believe He answers?

SECOND PERSON: He always does.

THIRD PERSON: It might be yes, or it might be no.

FIRST PERSON: Or it might be wait.

SECOND PERSON: Or He might have a better idea.

THIRD PERSON: He usually does.

FIRST PERSON: "Forgive us our debts as we forgive everyone who is indebted to us."

SECOND PERSON: Confession.

THIRD PERSON: You've got to tell Him when you make a mistake.

FIRST PERSON: He knows about them anyway.

SECOND PERSON: Lord, I really messed up today, yelling at the kids and Norman. I'm sorry.

THIRD PERSON: Confession leads to reconciliation, and reconciliation leads to peace of heart and mind.

FIRST PERSON: "And lead us not into temptation, but deliver us from evil."

SECOND PERSON: I don't get it. Why would God lead us into temptation?

THIRD PERSON: He doesn't, but He does allow us to be tempted, and we want to be able to recognize the temptations.

SECOND PERSON: Like to cheat on my income tax, or overcharge a customer, or to tell a lie because the truth hurts.

THIRD PERSON: You've got the idea.

FIRST PERSON: "For thine is the kingdom and the power and the glory forever."

SECOND PERSON: Remember who's in charge.

THIRD PERSON: And remember He loves you.

FIRST PERSON: So pray with joy.

SECOND PERSON: "Our Father who art in heaven..."

LIGHTS

59

The Answers Are Here

Topic:
Prayer

Theme:
God is faithful. He always answers prayer; it's just not always in a way we expect.

Scripture:
1 John 5:14,15
James 4:2,3

Characters:
Four People who represent God's answers:
　First Woman (disappointed but peace-filled)
　Man (relieved by God's answer)
　Student (a little disappointed emotionally with God's
　　answer, but intellectually understands)
　Second Woman (overjoyed with God's response)

Four People enter mechanically and line up behind microphone.

FIRST PERSON: We're here representing the four ways God answers prayer. I'm "Yes," the answer you always hope to receive. *(Steps to back and Second Person steps up.)*

SECOND PERSON: I'm "No," the unpopular one. *(Steps to the back and THIRD PERSON steps up.)*

THIRD PERSON: I'm "Wait a while," definitely not as popular as "Yes," but better than "No." *(Steps to the back and #4 steps up.)*

FOURTH PERSON: And I'm here representing, "I've got a better idea."

FIRST PERSON: We're here to be sure you understand that God always answers prayer, whether it be "Yes"...

SECOND PERSON: ..."No"...

THIRD PERSON: ..."Wait a while"...

FOURTH PERSON: ...or, "I've got a better idea."

(The Four People turn diagonally and look stage left where a woman is standing alone.)

WOMAN: My husband and I decided it was time to look for a house. So we did and we found this *perfect* little house: four bedrooms, three baths, it had a garbage disposal, a trash compactor, even an automatic garage door opener. It had all the luxuries I'd ever dreamed of. But we decided we'd better pray about it. So we did, and before too long we both realized it just wasn't the right time to buy it. Interest rates are so high. *(Freezes, then exits as Third Person steps out.)*

THIRD PERSON: She and her husband received "Wait." It doesn't mean that they won't ever live in a house. It just means the time wasn't right to buy that house. *(Gets back in line as attention turns to Man.)*

MAN: I've always wanted a Datsun 280 ZX turbo. When my old Plymouth died, I thought, "Now's my chance to have my dream car." So I prayed about it, and you won't believe what happened. I decided to get a moped. After all, my job is only two miles away, and I *really* couldn't have afforded the payments on the Z. A moped is more than I need. *(Freezes then exits as Fourth Person steps out.)*

FOURTH PERSON: God had a better idea. It was more practical and proved to make the man much happier. *(Gets back in line; attention turns to Student, stage left.)*

STUDENT: I made this decision to go to Colorado State University. There is snow skiing in the winter, backpacking in spring and summer, not to mention water skiing, horseback riding, and white water rafting. I mean, what better place to get an education? Then I started praying about my decision, and I realized I wasn't going there to get educated, but recreated. *(Freezes then exits as Second Person steps out.)*

SECOND PERSON: She got the big "n-o, no." Among other things, her motives were wrong. *(Gets back in line as attention turns to Second Woman, stage left.)*

LADY: The most wonderful thing happened to me! I got offered two jobs. But I was really having difficulty deciding which one to take. I mean, it's not every day you get offered two jobs. So I prayed about it. And I really felt at peace about which job I should take. Boy, am I excited. I know I made the right decision. *(Freezes as First Person steps out.)*

FIRST PERSON: She got me, the "Yes," the one you always wish for. But remember, whether it be "Yes"...

SECOND PERSON: ..."No"...

THIRD PERSON: ..."Wait a while"...

FOURTH PERSON: ...or "I've got a better idea"...

FIRST PERSON: God *will* answer.

LIGHTS

60
The Little Pew

Topic:
Prayer

Theme:
One of the most important things to remember when we are praying is that God is in charge and that He loves us.

Scripture:
1 Thessalonians 5:17
Ephesians 6:18
Luke 18:10-17

Characters:
Mary, a theological seven year old
Sara, a skeptical seven year old
Rachael, an average seven year old

Three children are in church. Mary is on her knees with eyes closed. She peeks out.

MARY: You don't have your eyes closed.

SARA: So what?

MARY: So you can't pray unless your eyes are closed.

RACHAEL: Yes, you can. My dad prays when he's driving to work and *his* eyes are open.

SARA: Well, what does he pray about?

RACHAEL: I don't know.

SARA: *(To Mary)* Does your dad pray?

MARY: I'm not sure. He says he's going to, but then he goes and lies down on the couch and closes his eyes and in a couple of minutes he's snoring. Can you pray when you snore?

RACHAEL: I don't think so.

MARY: How come you don't kneel when you pray?

RACHAEL: I don't know.

MARY: Well, I think you should. It helps a person remember how big God is.

SARA: How big is He?

MARY: My mom says He's big enough to help me with any problem I'll ever have.

SARA: Well, I don't pray.

MARY: Why?

SARA: Because it's stupid. Why would God talk with a little kid like me?

RACHAEL: Because He loves you, dummy.

MARY: Anybody who can put the whole world together and keep it going is pretty darn smart. And the way I've got it figured, growing up in today's world, I'm going to need all the help I can get. So I talk to Him alot.

SARA: What do you talk to Him about?

MARY: Everything and anything.

SARA: You mean He knows *everything?*

RACHAEL: Yep.

SARA: Maybe I should give it a try. Life's tough when you're seven.

LIGHTS

61
Colored Glass

Topic:
Purpose

Theme:
In all circumstances there are ways to honor and glorify God.

Scripture:
1 Corinthians 10:31
Romans 8:28

Characters:
Optimist
Pessimist
Realist

Props:
rose-colored sunglasses
dark sunglasses
newspaper

Three people are sitting at a bus stop. Optimist wears rose-colored glasses. Realist sits in the middle, reading a newspaper. Pessimist is wearing dark glasses.

OPTIMIST: Did you read about the ferry disaster?

PESSIMIST: It's terrible, absolutely terrible.

OPTIMIST: No, it isn't. God works all things together for good, for those who love him.

PESSIMIST: Well, obviously those people didn't. They were all sinners and God was punishing them. It's horrible, absolutely terrible, and *we'll* probably be next.

OPTIMIST: Speak for yourself. God loves me and I love Him. He's not going to let anything bad happen to me.

REALIST: Oh, really? Well, I love Him and bad things have happened to me.

OPTIMIST: *(Unwaveringly optimistic)* That's not how it works. All things work together for good.

REALIST: Well, believe it or not, I have problems.

OPTIMIST: That's not possible.

PESSIMIST: Of course it's possible. "For those whom the Lord loves He disciplines." Life's terrible, absolutely awful, and that's the way it's *supposed* to be.

REALIST: It's not terrible, but I do have some problems.

OPTIMIST: But Jesus came that we might have life and have life abundantly. You're not supposed to have problems. It's just *not* possible.

REALIST: Are you telling me you don't have *any* problems?

OPTIMIST: That's right. God is working everything together for good in my life.

REALIST: You could still have problems.

PESSIMIST: All He's doing for me is making my life miserable. He's responsible for me losing my job, my car breaking down, a filling falling out of my tooth, and my cat getting sick. It's terrible, absolutely terrible.

REALIST: I think you're underestimating and misunderstanding God.

PESSIMIST and OPTIMIST: *(Simultaneously lowering their glasses)* Oh, really?

REALIST: I don't think you're letting God be God. You're limiting what He does and doesn't do in your life, and that's not your job.

OPTIMIST: And what is our job?

REALIST: Well, I think it's to honor Him, and to glorify Him in whatever circumstance we're in.

OPTIMIST: You mean good or...

PESSIMIST: ...bad?

REALIST: That's right.

PESSIMIST: That's a radical concept.

OPTIMIST: Totally.

LIGHTS

62
Time Out

Topic:
Quiet Times

Theme:
God desires that people spend time with Him. He has given us the Bible, through which He communicates. However, we must make the time to read it.

Scripture:
Psalms 119:105
Luke 11:28
Hebrews 4:12

Characters:
Person
Voice of Bible

Props:
Bible

A Bible is center stage. Person walks in, obviously in a hurry. Looks at watch, then at Bible, then at watch again. Takes a couple of steps, then thinks better of it, picks up Bible, opens it to any page, closes eyes, picks a verse, reads it out loud, and closes the Bible.)

PERSON: Thanks, God.

BIBLE: *(Whispers)* Time out.

(Person looks around.)

BIBLE: *(Whispering again)* Time out.

PERSON: Who said that?

BIBLE: I did.

PERSON:Who?

BIBLE: Your Bible.

(Person picks up Bible, looks it over, shakes it.)

BIBLE: Hey, take it easy.

PERSON:*(Matter-of-factly)* Bibles don't talk.

BIBLE: Of course they do.

PERSON: *(Looks at Bible, shrugs)* Why'd you call "time out"? I mean, it's not like I'm giving up on reading or anything. It's just, well, I don't have time today and, well, to be perfectly honest, it *is* getting a little old. I mean, I talk and talk and talk to God but I don't get any answers. It's like talking to a brick wall.

BIBLE: Wait a minute. You're not supposed to do all the talking.

PERSON: I'm not?

BIBLE: No. God wants to talk to you, too.

PERSON: I haven't heard Him interrupting.

BIBLE: That's because you weren't listening; you were too busy talking.

PERSON: You mean God doesn't just want me to talk to Him? He wants to talk to me, too?

BIBLE: Right.

PERSON: But how?

BIBLE: You'll see Him working in your life, and He'll speak to you through me.

PERSON: *(Protesting)* But this is the first time you've ever said anything.

BIBLE: No. It's the first time you've ever heard anything. I've been trying to talk to you every time you open me up. I've got lots of advice for you, *and* encouragement, *and* support. You've just got to listen.

PERSON: I didn't know you were here to help. *(Looks at watch.)* Maybe I do have a few minutes to spend with God today. Do you think He'll speak to me? *(No response.)* Do you? *(No response; person looks around.)* I guess He already has. *(Opens Bible.)*

LIGHTS

63
Code 2106

Topic:
Relationships

Theme:
In order for our relationships to be effective, we must work at them. We must be willing to be vulnerable if we are to gain the benefits of a good relationship.

Scripture:
Hebrews 10:23-25
1 Thessalonians 5:11
Ephesians 4:25

Characters:
First Person
Second Person
Policeman

Props: (Optional)
Lone Ranger masks for First and Second Person
police hat
whistle
handcuffs

First and Second Person wear Lone Ranger masks.Their conversation is stilted and superficial.

FIRST PERSON: Hi, how you doing?

SECOND PERSON: Fine.

FIRST PERSON: How's your day been?

SECOND PERSON: Great.

FIRST PERSON: Anything I can help you with?

SECOND PERSON: Nope. How about you? How you doing?

FIRST PERSON: Fine.

SECOND PERSON: Well, I guess that's about all there is to say.

FIRST PERSON: I guess so.

SECOND PERSON: It was nice talking to you.

FIRST PERSON: You, too.

(Policeman enters, blowing whistle, carrying handcuffs.)

POLICEMAN: Hold it!

FIRST PERSON: What'd we do?

SECOND PERSON: We were just talking.

POLICEMAN: Is that what you call it? I call it a violation of Code 2106. *(Putting handcuffs on them)* You two are under arrest for impersonating a relationship.

SECOND PERSON: What do you mean? We just had a great conversation.

POLICEMAN: That was not a "great" conversation. You didn't tell each other anything about what was happening in your lives.

FIRST PERSON: We did so.

POLICEMAN: *(To First Person)* You didn't tell what the doctor said about your blood pressure.

SECOND PERSON: What'd the doctor say?

POLICEMAN: *(To Second Person)* And you didn't tell what happened with your boyfriend.

FIRST PERSON: What happened?

SECOND PERSON: Never mind.

POLICEMAN: You are not working at your relationship, and if you are not careful, the charge will be changed to wrongful death of a relationship.

SECOND PERSON: Now, wait just a minute. I want to see a lawyer.

POLICEMAN: If you care, you'll start sharing life with one another. You'll let God use you to love each other. You'll look at each other's point of view and be honest about your weaknesses and your strengths. That's what a relationship needs to keep growing.

FIRST PERSON: *(To Policeman)* Could I talk to you a moment alone? *(First Person whispers to Policeman)* If I tell what's really going on, what I'm really like, she won't like me. I've got to tell her what I think she wants to hear so she'll like me and we can still be friends.

SECOND PERSON: *(Has obviously overheard the conversation)* That's not true. I'd like you no matter what.

FIRST PERSON: No, you wouldn't; not if you knew.

SECOND PERSON: Knew what? Knew that you didn't really like Mel Gibson, and that you just pretended to because I do?

FIRST PERSON: *(Taking off mask)* How'd you know that?

SECOND PERSON: I just did.

FIRST PERSON: Well, I like you even though you have a bad temper.

SECOND PERSON: *(Taking off mask, innocently)* Who, me?

FIRST PERSON: But would you like me if you knew I liked peanut butter and pickles on rye?

SECOND PERSON: You do? I like it, too. And there's a great little restaurant around the corner where we can get peanut butter and pickles on rye. It's their special. *(To policeman)* Could you please unhook us?

POLICEMAN: OK. But I don't ever want to catch you impersonating a relationship again.

FIRST PERSON: No problem.

LIGHTS

64
Big Business

Topic:
Religion

Theme:
Religion can often take the place of our relationship with the Lord.

Scripture:
John 3

Characters:
Sue
Sam

Props:
a telegram

Two business people have just received a telegram stating that their business is being shut down.

SUE: I don't understand why He sent this.

SAM: Obviously, He couldn't get through to us any other way. This telegram says He's been trying for months. I guess we haven't been listening.

SUE: Shhh! We don't want to let that information get out. People will call us hypocrites.

SAM: Don't you see it doesn't matter? He's closing down our office.

SUE: But that isn't fair. Our business is booming. We've got more people doing more things for Him than ever before. We've got Bible studies every hour, prayer chains, religious aerobic classes, car washes, laundromats, and grocery stores. Just last week we sold a chocolate chip cookie franchise to a group of Christians who'll make a fish out of chocolate chips on every cookie.

SAM: Apparently He isn't impressed with the fact that we turned our little Bible study into a multi-million-dollar industry. And to be perfectly honest, I'm tired of all this running around anyway.

SUE: I'll admit it was a lot more fun when we first started. It's just big business now.

SAM: Big business, big money, and big ministry. I mean we've got people who are willing to pay to pray.

SUE: Maybe that's why He's shutting us down. Maybe He didn't like us charging people to do things for Him.

SAM: They were probably supposed to want to do them on their own rather than be motivated by our million-dollar advertising campaign.

SUE: You know, I can't remember the last time I sat down and talked to the Lord just because I wanted to.

SAM: That's because you've been so busy enrolling people in Bible studies, encouraging them to go to prayer meetings, signing them up for aerobic classes and making appointments for car washes.

SUE: Well, I'll have plenty of free time now. But I don't know how to begin.

SAM: Maybe we could start with a small Bible study.

SUE: But that's so simple. Besides, we know all that stuff.

SAM: I think we've forgotten it. If we really knew it, we wouldn't be out of work.

SUE: Right.

LIGHTS

65
The Beginning of the End

Topic:
End Times

Theme:
The book of Revelation gives several signs that enable us to recognize the beginning of the end times. Knowledge of these signs can help us be aware and warn others of the end of the world.

Scripture:
Revelation 6:1-8

Characters:
Realist
Pessimist
Optimist (cheerful, always smiling, has a unrealistic view of life)
Christian

Four people with different perspectives have been stuck in an elevator for two-and-a-half hours.

REALIST: It's already been two and a half hours. How can it take two and a half hours to fix an elevator?

PESSIMIST: They are never coming.

OPTIMIST: They probably haven't noticed the elevator is stuck yet.

REALIST: I'm sure they've noticed.

PESSIMIST: They don't care.

OPTIMIST: *(Reassuringly)* Of course they care. I'm sure someone will be here any minute.

REALIST: You've been saying that for the last two and a half hours.

OPTIMIST: *(Undaunted)* Every time I say it, we are a minute closer to them coming.

PESSIMIST: Or a minute closer to dying.

REALIST: I doubt that.

PESSIMIST: It's probably the end of the world and everyone has been obliterated.

REALIST: I don't think so.

CHRISTIAN: The end of the world hasn't come yet. Certain things have to happen before the world ends.

REALIST: Like what?

CHRISTIAN: There will be wars and famine. The world economy will collapse.

PESSIMIST: *(To himself)* I knew it. I knew it.

CHRISTIAN: There will be massive persecution of Christians and probably all-out nuclear war.

PESSIMIST: That's worse than I ever imagined.

CHRISTIAN: Then there will be a break in the action. God will give everyone a chance to believe in Him before the final battle.

REALIST: The final battle?

OPTIMIST: At least we have a chance to repent before the end.

PESSIMIST: Only if we haven't been killed by the wars and famine.

REALIST: *(To Christian)* How do we even know what you're saying is true?

CHRISTIAN: You can read it for yourself.

REALIST: *(A little sarcastically)* Where? In the Bible?

CHRISTIAN: As a matter of fact, yes.

OPTIMIST: When we get out of here, I'm going to read it. It sounds great!

REALIST: The end of the world sounds great?

OPTIMIST: No, but knowing about it would be. Then a person could be prepared. Hey, the elevator is moving. We're saved.

CHRISTIAN: Temporarily.

(Pessimist walks out, muttering about the wars and famines. Optimist leaves, talking about reading about the end of the world. Realist walks out, then comes back to Christian.)

REALIST: Where can I read about that again? I want to be prepared, just in case.

LIGHTS

66
The Museum

Topic:
End Times

Theme:
The book of Revelation shows that some day there will be one world government, one religion, and one economy. Many people will be deceived into thinking that that is the answer to a world in crisis. Obviously, it is not. Jesus will return. He will be victorious. He is the only way to God, the Father, and the only—the ultimate—solution to a world in crisis.

Scripture:
Revelation 12:18

Characters:
First Person (humanist)
Second Person (most undecided philosophical of the four)
Third Person (nominally interested in Christianity; doesn't take Bible literally)
Fourth Person (Christian)

Four people are looking at pictures in a museum.

FIRST PERSON: *(Pointing to picture)* Now *that* is a great picture. It really symbolizes what I have always thought should happen.

FOURTH PERSON: What do you mean?

FIRST PERSON: I've always thought that people of all religions should unite and with one effort bring peace to the world. If Jesus, Mohammed, Buddha, and all the rest actually sat down together like in that picture, we could solve a lot of the world's problems.

SECOND PERSON: But we'd need one world government to put all the religious ideas into action.

THIRD PERSON: *(Enthusiastically)* And then we could have one world economy and we wouldn't have to worry about inflation.

FIRST PERSON: There'd be one world leader.

SECOND PERSON: It sounds like we've come up with quite a plan.

THIRD PERSON: Come to think of it, I think I remember reading about one world religion, one world government, and one world economy in a book. *(Trying to think of it)* It's called Revelation. It's part of the Bible.

FIRST PERSON: Maybe that's where the artist got his inspiration.

FOURTH PERSON: I don't think he finished reading the Book then.

FIRST PERSON: Why do you say that?

FOURTH PERSON: He wouldn't have put Jesus in the picture.

SECOND PERSON: Why not?

FOURTH PERSON: Jesus isn't like other religious leaders. He's the only one who ever claimed to be God. He's the only one who sacrificed himself for us, and he's the only one who was resurrected. And he's the only answer for a world in crisis.

THIRD PERSON: Then he'll be in charge of the one world government, right?

FOURTH PERSON: Not according to the book of Revelation. There will be one world government and one world religion, but he won't be a part of it. He will bring an end to it, though, when he returns.

SECOND PERSON: Really?

FOURTH PERSON: Yeah, when he comes back, he's coming back for good, and *he'll* be in charge forever.

SECOND PERSON: That artist should have read the whole book.

FIRST PERSON: Maybe we should, too.

SECOND PERSON: Yeah. Hey, look at this one over here. It's by the same artist. It's called "THE END."

LIGHTS

67
A World Apart

Topic:
Sanctification

Theme:
God's will for us includes that we be sanctified. This means we must: 1) avoid sexual immorality, 2) be holy and honorable with our bodies, and 3) practice honorable business ethics. The world, in contrast to the Christian, participates in all of these unsanctified activities. We, as Christians, must set ourselves apart from these worldly activities.

Scripture:
1 Thessalonians 4:1-8

Characters:
First, Third, and Fifth Persons (represent the world)
Second, Fourth, and Sixth Persons (represent Christianity)

Six people are walking in a circle symbolic of the world.

FIRST PERSON: There's nothing wrong with premarital sex.

THIRD PERSON: Or extramarital sex.

FIFTH PERSON: Everyone else is doing it.

FIRST PERSON: Don't be a prude.

THIRD PERSON: Everybody else is doing it.

FIFTH PERSON: It doesn't hurt anybody.

FIRST PERSON: Besides, it's a lot of fun.

SECOND PERSON: *(Steps out of circle)* I can't.

(First, Third, and Fifth Persons shrug their shoulders, continue walking.)

THIRD PERSON: What's a little cocaine?

FIFTH PERSON: Drinking is perfectly legal.

FIRST PERSON: There isn't anything wrong with getting a buzz.

THIRD PERSON: Besides, it's my body; I can do what I want with it.

FOURTH PERSON: *(Stepping out of the circle)* That's not for me.

(First, Third, and Fifth Persons shrug their shoulders and keep walking.)

FIFTH PERSON: There's no reason to report my tips. The IRS has no way of finding out how much they were.

FIRST PERSON: My dad takes us out to dinner on the company card all the time.

THIRD PERSON: Sure, I add an extra hour of labor to my customers' bill. They never even notice, so it probably doesn't make any difference to them.

FIFTH PERSON: Like I always say, look out for Number One *(points to self)*.

SIXTH PERSON: *(Stepping out of the circle)* Well, I'm not going to.

FIRST PERSON: Where are you going?

THIRD PERSON: Don't you want to be a part of the real world?

FIFTH PERSON: Don't you want to be on top of things?

SECOND PERSON: Not if it means doing what you're doing.

FOURTH PERSON: We're supposed to be different.

FIRST PERSON: From what?

SIXTH PERSON: From you.

THIRD PERSON: Says who?

SECOND PERSON: God.

FIRST PERSON: Are you trying to be holy or something?

FOURTH PERSON: Exactly.

THIRD PERSON: Then you'll never be a success.

FIFTH PERSON: You'll never amount to anything.

SIXTH PERSON: Maybe not by your definition, but by His *(points up)* I will.

FIRST PERSON: Well, don't go spreading *your* definition around.

SECOND PERSON: Why not?

THIRD PERSON: The world wouldn't be like it is if everybody lived like you.

SECOND, FOURTH, and SIXTH PERSONS: Exactly.

LIGHTS

68
The Spitting Image

Topic:
Self-Image

Theme:
We are God's creation. We must remember this and act accordingly if we are to live the way God intends us to.

Scripture:
Ephesians 2:8-10

Characters:
Mom
Dad

Props:
Wall Street Journal
catalog
two coffee mugs
flour (for dust)
two Bibles

Dad is reading the Wall Street Journal. An exhausted Mom enters with coffee cups.

MOM: They are finally asleep. Now for a special moment in our life. (*She hands Dad a cup of coffee.*)

DAD: How did you finally get them to sleep?

MOM: I had to read little Carl an article from the *Wall Street Journal.*

DAD: *(Proudly)* That's my boy.

MOM: He's the spitting image of you.

DAD: What'd you read to Chrissy?

MOM: It's not important.

DAD: Come on, what'd you read her?

MOM: I'd rather not say.

DAD: What'd you read her?

MOM: The Nordstrom's sale catalog.

DAD: You realize you're raising a shopaholic?

MOM: *(Rationalizing)* Well, you're raising a Wall Street tycoon.

DAD: Why are we trying to create them in our image?

MOM: I don't know. We're not that great.

DAD: What are the alternatives?

MOM: Well, we *were* created in God's image.

DAD: But we don't act like it.

MOM: We could try. After all, God considers us important. He allowed his own Son to die for us.

DAD: I don't know if we could do it. We'd have to be obedient and caring and loving. We'd have to try to follow God's guidelines for living.

MOM: But isn't that what we want for them? It'll certainly give them a better life than a stock portfolio or a designer wardrobe. It'll give them security for eternity.

DAD: So much for a special moment in our lives. Actually, it was special; it just isn't going to make things easy.

(Dad puts down his Wall Street Journal, *blows dust off Bible, and sits down again. Mom puts down Nordstrom catalog, blows dust off Bible, and sits down to read it.)*

LIGHTS

69

Forgiven, but Still Feeling Guilty

Topic:
Sin

Theme:
When Christians sin, they must confess and repent. Then they are forgiven and have no reason for guilt. However, they do have to endure the consequences.

Scripture:
1 John 1:9
Colossians 3:25
Psalms 103:12

Characters:
Daughter
Mother
Sin
Guilt
Consequences

Props: (Optional)
2-3 dresses lying on a bench or table

DAUGHTER: *(Looking in closet for something to wear on important date tonight. She is nervous and irritable.)* Mom, where's my red silk dress?

MOTHER: *(Offstage)* Look in your closet.

DAUGHTER: *(Annoyed that her mother would give such an obvious answer)* It's not here.

MOTHER: *(Entering)* Then it's probably still at the cleaners.

DAUGHTER: *(Blows up)* The cleaners? But I wanted to wear it tonight. I've got a date with *Bill*. What am I going to do?

MOTHER: You'll just have to wear something else.

DAUGHTER: But I was counting on wearing that dress.

MOTHER: I'm sorry. I'm not a mind reader, honey. I didn't know you needed that dress.

DAUGHTER: Well, you should have. Mothers are *supposed* to know things like that. They're supposed to know what you want to wear, what you like to eat, when you want to talk, and when you want to be left alone. What kind of mother are you, anyway?

MOTHER: *(A little hurt)* I think I'll take that as a hint and leave you alone.

(Daughter mumbles something about having such a stupid mother; Sin, Guilt, and Consequences enter.)

DAUGHTER: Who are you and what are you doing in my room?

SIN: You invited us here.

DAUGHTER: I most certainly did not. I have a date with Bill tonight.

GUILT: So?

DAUGHTER: So get out and leave me alone. I've got to get dressed.

CONSEQUENCES: Not until we finish our business.

DAUGHTER: *(Caught a little off guard)* What business? I don't even know you.

SIN: (Putting out hand) Hi, I'm Sin.

DAUGHTER: *(Hesitantly takes hand)* Sin?

SIN: I'm here because of the way you treated your mother.

DAUGHTER: *(Defensively)* So I got a little mad.

SIN: You were angry and irrational.

GUILT: Not to mention rude and disrespectful.

DAUGHTER: And who are you?

GUILT: I'm Guilt. I always follow Sin. *(Proudly)* I help you feel bad when you make mistakes.

DAUGHTER: Oh. *(Thinks a second.)* Well, I suppose you two do have a point. I wasn't very nice to my mom, and it really wasn't her fault.

SIN: You hurt her feelings.

GUILT: *(Rubbing it in)* Pretty bad.

DAUGHTER: *(Feeling a little bad)* I did get a little carried away. But what can I do about it now?

SIN: First you should confess it. Tell God you're sorry for the way you treated your mom.

GUILT: And then you can apologize to her.

DAUGHTER: And then?

SIN: And then we'll leave.

GUILT: There won't be any reason for us to stay around.

DAUGHTER: *(Relieved)* Good.

SIN: *(Exiting with Guilt)* But I'm sure we'll see you later.

DAUGHTER: *(Looks oddly at Consequences)* What about you?

CONSEQUENCES: Oh, I'll be around for a while. I'm the consequences.

DAUGHTER: Consequences?

CONSEQUENCES: Of your sin.

DAUGHTER: *(Protesting)* But I said I'd confess and apologize.

CONSEQUENCES: Your mom was really hurt by what you said. She may not be able to forget it as easy as you.

DAUGHTER: I never looked at it like that before. I guess I need God to help me make things right with my mom as much as I need forgiveness. *(Thinks a second.)* Do you think flowers would help?

CONSEQUENCES: That would certainly be a start.

LIGHTS

70
The Gift

Topic:
Spiritual Gifts

Theme:
God gives every believer a spiritual gift. Once believers realize that God has given them a gift, it is their responsibility to discover and use their spiritual gift(s).

Scripture:
Ephesians 4:11-14
1 Corinthians 14:1-12
Romans 12:4-8

Characters:
Laurie (loves to talk and loves her imaginary cat)

Props:
wrapped package

LAURIE: Bootsie! Here Kitty! *(The pretend kitty enters.)* That a boy. How was your day, Bootsie? Catch any mice? You're a good kitty. I had a great day, Bootsie! You know, I had no idea that when I decided to work at pleasing God, it would end up pleasing me. *(Sits down.)* I thought I'd be miserable, but I'm not. I thought it would be hard to read the Bible every day, and sometimes it *is*, but I'm learning so much. God is doing a lot for me. It's pretty exciting, Bootsie, and now that I'm going to church regularly and meeting other believers, I'm even more inclined to do what God wants. *(Thinks a second.)* It's kind of like peer pressure, you know what I mean, Bootsie? *(Looks at cat.)* No, I guess you wouldn't. *(Spots present.)* What's this? A present? Bootsie, how did this get here? It's not my birthday. *(Looks at tag.)* It's for me—from God! You won't believe this, Bootsie, but I just learned about spiritual gifts. They're gifts that God gives to every believer. This is probably mine; it's here. I can hardly believe it. That's got to be more than a coincidence, Bootsie. I'm kind of scared to open it. I mean, once I open it, I'll be stuck. But then again, it might be something really great and then I'll be sorry if I don't open it. So I guess I should find out what it is, Bootsie. *(Thinks a second.)* After all, it *is* from God and it *is* for me. Whatever it is, it'll be exactly what He wants me to have. I'll tell you what, you take off the ribbon and I'll take off the paper.

LIGHTS

71
Guardian Angel

Topic:
Stress

Theme:
Every one of us experiences times in our lives when circumstances seem overwhelming. To handle them God's way, we must: 1) pray, 2) look at the positive things in our life, and 3) act accordingly.

Scripture:
Philippians 4:6,7
Matthew 6:24
Ephesians 6:18

Characters:
Person (overwhelmed by negative circumstances)
Guardian Angel (sent to help person discover the best way to handle problems)

PERSON: *(Heavy sigh)* I got a bill from the dentist today, $750. I am still paying off brakes for the car and now it's my teeth, too. It's always something. You know, I think it's a universal law that if it's not one thing, it's another. If it's not the chicken pox, the dog's sick; if it's not the dishwasher breaking down, my in-laws are coming to visit. If the car is running OK, then an appliance breaks down. I just wish I could do something about it.

GUARDIAN ANGEL: *(Suddenly appears)* You can.

PERSON: *(Surprised)* Who are you?

GUARDIAN ANGEL: You don't recognize me?

PERSON: No. Should I?

GUARDIAN ANGEL: Yes, I'm a guardian angel.

PERSON: *(Impressed)* You mean you are one of those people who rides around in the subways and keeps people from getting mugged?

GUARDIAN ANGEL: Not that kind of angel. The real thing.

PERSON: Really?

GUARDIAN ANGEL: Yes, and there are things you can do about stress.

PERSON: There are?

GUARDIAN ANGEL: *(Knowing none of the following people have the answers, but wanting Person to admit it)* Sure. You could deal with it like your friend, Ollie.

PERSON: Oh no. Ollie ignores his problems. He makes believe they don't exist and prays like crazy they'll go away.

GUARDIAN ANGEL: What about Theresa?

PERSON: No. She drowns her problems in pina coladas.

GUARDIAN ANGEL: How about Bradford?

PERSON: He never relaxes; just bulldozes his way through anything.

GUARDIAN ANGEL: Well, what about Ethel?

PERSON: She's always running away from her problems.

GUARDIAN ANGEL: There's another option.

PERSON: What is it?

GUARDIAN ANGEL: Handle it God's way.

PERSON: How?

GUARDIAN ANGEL: First, deal with your feelings; pray about them. Second, think positively; always look for the good. And third, act accordingly.

PERSON: And that'll bring me peace?

GUARDIAN ANGEL: It sure will.

PERSON: *(To himself)* So I need to deal with my feelings, think positively, and act accordingly. *(Looking toward Guardian Angel, who has disappeared)* Hey, th— Where'd you go? *(Looks up.)* Thanks.

LIGHTS

72
The Stress Battle

Topic:
Stress

Theme:
God does not want us to be anxious about anything. However, Satan does. At times it seems Satan is bombarding us with reasons to worry. And he may be doing just that.

Scripture:
Philippians 4:6,7
Matthew 6:25-34

Characters:
Helper
Stress Pest

Props:
children's blocks

Stress Pest is placing blocks on stage.

STRESS PEST: These stress-producing stumbling blocks will make this Christian incapable of influencing her world today. She'll be crabby, nagging, complaining, short-tempered, rude, and diabolically unpleasant.

Here is the stack of bills she'll have to pay; here's the note Billy will bring home from his teacher; this is her dentist appointment; and to top things off, tonight is her eight-year-old's slumber party. *(Sits down pompously.)* I love watching humans become immobilized by stress.

HELPER: Then you're in the wrong place.

STRESS PEST: What do you mean? This is a *surefire* stress-filled day.

HELPER: Not for this human. She reads the "Instruction Book."

STRESS PEST: *(A little worried)* Not Philippians!

HELPER: That's right. And she's prayed about all these stumbling blocks. She's told God her feelings and feels *his* peace.

STRESS PEST: I hate that word: peace.

HELPER: *(Picking up blocks and stacking them)* These stumbling blocks won't work on her.

STRESS PEST: *(Thinks a moment)* I'll get her. I'll use more stresses. She won't be able to follow the Philippians method forever. Sooner or later, she'll crack, and I'll be there to enjoy her failures.

HELPER: I don't think so.

STRESS PEST: What do you mean, "you don't think so"?

HELPER: She also knows when to *cease*. She and her husband know that they need time for themselves.

STRESS PEST: You mean she knows how to get God's "peace" and also "cease?"

HELPER: That's right.

STRESS PEST: But that's not fair. How can I get to her if she knows that?

HELPER: You can't. She and her husband will be spending a nice, quiet Saturday bike riding at the reservoir.

STRESS PEST: It sounds dreadful.

HELPER: It's just what they need.

STRESS PEST: Did she find that out in the Book, too?

HELPER: That's right.

STRESS PEST: Peace and Cease. That's disgusting. I think I'll find another human to bother. *(To audience)* Anyone interested in some stumbling blocks?

LIGHTS

Appendix A
Writing Three-Minute Sketches

So you think writing a sketch for your church worship service is a great idea. You have a dozen sharp pencils and several pads of paper. You sit down eager to begin. Then your mind goes blank. What do you write? How do you start?

First, you need to decide what the sketch is going to be about and what point or points you wish to make through the drama. These decisions will help you narrow down your subject matter. This is important because it gives the drama a focus. Without this focus, it is easy to say too much.

For example, let's say you decide you are going to write a drama about prayer. There are many different ways to approach this. You could focus the drama on how to pray, what prayer is, when to pray, how prayer is answered, or how Jesus prayed, just to mention a few.

Let's say you decide to write a drama on "how to pray." Once again, you must narrow the focus of your drama. There are many ways to pray, and it would be near to impossible to cover them all in one drama.

To determine exactly what you want to communicate about how to pray, I suggest you get your Bible and use it to help you. Look up your subject in the concordance. Choose a biblical reference about your subject that will be the underlying theme for your drama. Pray that God will illuminate a truth to you so that you will be able to communicate it through the drama.

Continuing with the prayer example, let's say you use the concordance and refer in your Bible to Matthew 6:6-13:

> When you pray, go into your room, close the door and pray to your Father, who is unseen. Then your Father, who sees what is done in secret, will reward you. And when you pray, do not keep on babbling like pagans, for they think they will be heard because of their many words. Do not be like them, for your Father knows what you need before you ask him. This is how you should pray: "Our Father in heaven, hallowed be your name, your kingdom come, your will be done on earth as it is in heaven. Give us today our daily bread. Forgive us our debts, as we also have forgiven our debtors. And lead us not into temptation, but deliver us from the evil one" (New International Version).

From this scripture you decide that the points you want to make about prayer are:

1. Don't use meaningless repetition.
2. Acknowledge God's sovereignty and power.

There are many other truths about prayer in that passage, but you can't communicate them all in one three-minute drama.

Next, you need to brainstorm. Write down real-life situations where these biblical truths are evident. Then, write down real- life situations where this biblical truth is *not* evident. This list is generally longer.

If you can't think of any situations at all, don't be alarmed. More prayer is helpful here. Also, getting a drink of water, going for a walk, having a snack, or re-reading the scripture are all ways to allow your creative motor to start.

If you still can't think of anything, look at the "Script Ideas" on pages 247-249. Generally, looking at those locations and characters will give you an idea.

After deciding on a situation, try outlining it. Write out how the drama will begin, what will happen in the middle, and how it ends. Who are the characters? How will they make your point(s)?

Continuing with the prayer example, let's suppose you decide that children often naturally pray acknowledging God's sovereignty. Adults, on the other hand, often forget his sovereignty and resort to meaningless repetitious requests.

You imagine a father trying to fix a broken refrigerator. He is frustrated and upset. The mother is telling the father what to do. She is also mumbling prayers like "God help him, God be with us, God fix it, please fix it," when she is not griping at the father. The father is mad at his wife for telling him what to do, mad at the refrigerator for being broken, and mad at God for allowing refrigerators to be invented. The mother and father end up yelling at each other and leaving the room. Their child, who has been coloring, is left alone in the kitchen. The child offers a simple but sincere prayer. The prayer acknowledges God's power over all things. The child asks God to help his parents, and, if at all possible, to fix the refrigerator.

The child shows the right attitude in prayer, while the parents' attitude shows a lack of understanding of God and prayer.

Once you have an outline, you can begin to write the dialogue. Try to write like people talk. Use language that is easy to understand. Don't try to make something funny. As you cultivate your imagination about the situation, you will find plenty of humor inherent in the situation.

After you have a first draft, go back and edit it. Keep in mind the focus of your drama when you edit it. If you've gone off on any tangents, now is the time to take them out.

It's a good idea to wait until the next day to write a third draft. After being away from the drama you will come back with a clearer perspective. Then your third draft can be a final one.

Congratulations! You've written a drama!

Summary: Five Steps to Writing Your Own Three-Minute Drama

1. Decide on the biblical principle or truth you are trying to communicate.
2. Imagine a real-life situation where that biblical truth is evident and where it is not.
3. Outline the drama.
4. Write dialogue.
5. Rewrite and edit.

Appendix B
Nuts and Bolts of Producing A Sketch

Certain elements enable these sketches to be performed in a way that both communicates a message and entertains. These are the nuts and bolts of the three-minute drama. They include actors, a director, rehearsals, and props.

Finding people to perform the sketches is your first priority. You'll probably be surprised at how many people in your church have had experience in drama. However, as with anything new, these "closet actors" may be somewhat reluctant to volunteer. If you don't get volunteers right away, don't despair. Try a personal invitation to one or two of your friends. With a little coaxing, they'll probably be willing to help you out—at least once! After that, others will begin to get interested, and you'll have all the volunteers you need.

Once you have the people to perform the dramas, you'll need a director. The director is the person who coordinates the sketch. The director will tell people where to move, what tone of voice to use, and when to use a prop. It is best for the director not to be in the sketch. Then the director can objectively view the actions and performances of those in the drama.

Now that there is a director and actors, you'll need to rehearse. In our ministry we have always rehearsed for about thirty-five minutes before our service actually begins. The director and the people who are in the drama must come *prepared* to the rehearsal. The actors must have their lines memorized before they arrive, and the director must know where, when, and why he or she wants people to move. When everyone comes to the rehearsal prepared, it will run efficiently and effectively.

Although this rehearsal schedule works for our drama ministry, it may not work for everyone. Experiment with your rehearsal time until you find a schedule that suits your needs.

Props and costumes can be a real asset to a sketch if they are used appropriately. They should not be added just because they are cute. They should help create the mood and setting of the drama. Following is a list of props I have found to be very useful:

briefcases
hats (all kinds)
magazines
newspapers
shopping bags
suitcases
sunglasses
telephone(s)
television

Appendix C
Script Ideas: Characters and Settings

Characters

angel
athlete
boss
businessperson
butler
child
construction worker
daughter
dentist
doctor
employee
father
florist
garbageperson
gardener
God
husband
lawyer
maid
minister
mother
musician

nurse
patient
person
police officer
salesclerk
secretary
son
steward
student
teacher
teenager
truck driver
used-car salesman
wife
zookeeper

Add your own ideas for characters here:

_____

_____

_____

_____

_____

Settings

airplane
bus
business meeting
cafeteria
car
cemetary

church
concert
construction site
dentist's office
dinner table
doctor's office
elevator
heaven
lawyer's office
library
museum
park
picnic
planetarium
school
sporting event
subway
train
zoo

Add your own ideas for settings here:

_____

_____

_____

_____

_____

Scripture Index

Topic Index